YORK NOTES

General Editors: Professor A.N. Jeffares (*University of Stirling*) & Professor Suheil Bushrui (*American University of Beirut*)

Homer

THE ODYSSEY

Notes by Robin Sowerby

MA PH D (CAMBRIDGE)
Lecturer, Department English Studies,
University of Stirling

LONGMAN
YORK PRESS

YORK PRESS
Immeuble Esseily, Place Riad Solh, Beirut.

LONGMAN GROUP UK LIMITED
Longman House, Burnt Mill, Harlow,
Essex CM20 2JE, England
Associated companies, branches and representatives
throughout the world

First published 1986
Third impression 1990

ISBN 0-582-03353-5

Produced by Longman Group (FE) Ltd.
Printed in Hong Kong

Contents

Part 1

Introduction

The Homeric Question

Nothing is known for certain about the authorship of the *Odyssey* or about its date and place of composition. Indeed all the circumstances surrounding the composition and early transmission of the Homeric poems are matters of surmise and controversy that together have come to be known as the Homeric Question. It is unlikely that a satisfactory solution to the problem that has perplexed scholars and critics alike in an acute form for nearly two centuries will now ever be found. The literature upon the subject is very considerable and all that can be done here is to indicate some of the main difficulties and to record the latest consensus of scholarly opinion. That consensus may be more apparent than real and at best can offer only a likely account.

The Homeric poems are the oldest surviving texts in Greek culture. There are no internal references to their author or to their origin and there are no other contemporary documents to throw light upon them. They exist in what is virtually an historical vacuum. Nor is there any reliable tradition about their origin in the earliest Greek literature following them. The Greeks all agree on the name 'Homer' and there is a persistent tradition that, like the bard Demodocus in the *Odyssey*, he was blind, but different views are recorded concerning his date and birthplace. Seven cities claimed to be the birthplace of Homer, the most favoured in antiquity being Chios and Smyrna, both in the region of Ionia in the eastern Aegean. The Greeks believed in the historical reality of the Trojan War, but they questioned the reliability of the Homeric version. According to some accounts he was a contemporary witness of events; according to others his poem was composed some time after the fall of Troy, an event which in any case was for the earliest Greek historians shrouded in the mists of pre-history.

Any consideration of the Homeric Question must begin with the picture of the Homeric bard in the *Odyssey*. There are two bards in the poem, Phemius, resident in the palace of Odysseus in Ithaca, and the blind Demodocus who resides in the palace of King Alcinous in Phaeacia which is visited by Odysseus in the course of his wanderings from Troy. Both bards have an honoured place and sing to the accompaniment of the lyre. Phemius sings of the woes inflicted on the Greeks returning from Troy (I, 326–7). Demodocus sings three short songs, the first of which is about a quarrel between the leading Greeks at the beginning of the Trojan story (VIII, 73–82). The second is a comic tale about the gods (VIII, 266–366). The third is at the request of Odysseus, who commends Demodocus for his truthfulness in faithfully recording the memory of the sufferings of the Greeks at Troy and asks him to sing of the Wooden Horse, the stratagem by which the Greeks took Troy. Demodocus being stirred by the god of song begins from the point at which the Greeks sailed away (line 500). He tells how the Trojans took the huge horse into the city thinking that the Greeks had departed, and how the Greeks hidden inside it came out at night and sacked the city (VIII, 487–520). The implication is that Demodocus knows many songs about gods and heroes and that in particular he knows the whole Trojan story which he can take up at any point. Moreover the bard faithfully transmits the memory of the great events of the past. Later in the poem Phemius boasts to Odysseus that he is self-taught and knows many different songs. The poet of the *Odyssey* and the *Iliad* must be a descendant of the Homeric bard he describes. But Demodocus and Phemius work on a small scale with single tales. There is no hint in either the *Odyssey* or *Iliad* of an occasion which could have prompted the composition of poems of such great length and scope.

How could the poems have been transmitted? Early literary sources report the existence of a guild who claimed to be the descendants of Homer called the Homeridae, who flourished in Chios and were devoted to the recitation of his poems. In addition there were other professional reciters of Homer's poetry called rhapsodes. Their existence is well attested, and they recited Homer's poetry from memory at public festivals and games where they competed with one another for prizes. Again it is difficult to imagine an occasion on which the poems might have been recited in their entirety.

It was the lack of any known occasion for poems of this length, together with the difficulty of explaining how poems of this length and artistic unity could have been composed without the aid of writing, that led the German Homeric scholar Friedrich Wolf (1759–1824) to raise the Homeric Question. It is not that Wolf denied the existence of 'Homer'. He believed that Homer had existed and had initiated the poems in their early form. But he declared in his *Prolegomena ad Homerum* of 1795 that the Homeric poems, as we know them, did not have a single author but had progressively evolved, as successive rhapsodes added and developed what had come down to them. Some ancient scholars known as the chorizontes or separators had believed that the *Odyssey* and *Iliad* were by different authors, and some ancient commentators had suspected that particular lines and even some episodes had been interpolated, but it was not until Wolf that unity of authorship in the individual poems was fundamentally questioned.

Wolf's theory arose primarily from a consideration of the external factors mentioned above. After him the poems themselves were rigorously analysed. Internal discrepancies and inconsistencies were seen to be evidence of multiple authorship. In this time even those who disagreed with Wolf's conclusions accepted that the Homeric poems had come into being gradually over a period of time, since it is apparent that like a rock face they contain various layers of material, some of which must be given a comparatively late date and some that belong to earlier time.

Archaeology and the Homeric poems

The ancient Greeks had believed in the substantial reality of Homer's world but in modern times students of Homer from the eighteenth century onwards tended to believe that the material world of Homer and the events he described were poetic fictions, until in the later part of the nineteenth century archaeologists began to reconstruct the early history of civilisation in the Mediterranean from the physical evidence provided by excavations. The most famous name in Homeric archaeology is that of the German scholar Heinrich Schliemann (1822–1890) who excavated what he believed to be the site of Troy at Hissarlik in northern Turkey in the early 1870s. His conviction that he had found Homer's Troy has been vindicated by all the subsequent research into the evidence. He later excavated Mycenae in 1876 and Tiryns in 1884 on the Greek mainland. Other places mentioned in Homer, notably Pylos, were investigated by other archaeologists. Shortly after 1900 Sir Arthur Evans (1851–1941) excavated Cnossus in Crete, and these early archaeological endeavours provided the foundation for new knowledge about ancient Greece in the period before literary records are available. This new knowledge has tended to suggest that the culture and events of the Homeric poems have some basis in historical truth.

The island of Crete is the earliest centre of civilisation in the Mediterranean. The remains at Cnossus show that the Bronze Age civilisation called Minoan (from Minos the mythical lawgiver of Crete) was highly developed and lasted from roughly 3000 to 1000BC. On mainland Greece, a Bronze Age civilisation centred upon royal palaces such as those excavated at Mycenae, Tiryns and Pylos developed somewhat later and lasted from 1580 to 1120BC. This civilisation is called Mycenaean from what seems to have been its most powerful centre, Mycenae. In the *Iliad* Agamemnon, leader of the Greek expedition to Troy and the most powerful of the Greek princes, comes from Mycenae which Homer calls 'rich in gold', 'broad streeted' and 'well built'. In the Catalogue of Ships in the second book of the *Iliad* the largest numbers come from Mycenae and Pylos.

The great house of the *Odyssey* bears a resemblance to Mycenaean palaces excavated on the main sites. The region in which the palace of Odysseus was located is thought to have been on the edge of Mycenaean civilisation. On both Thiaki, believed by the ancients and by many moderns to have been Homer's Ithaca, and on Leucas (now a promontory but possibly an island in remote antiquity) the other main rival for identification with Ithaca, there are Mycenaean remains.

A script known as Linear B on clay tablets found at Pylos, Mycenae and Cnossus establishes strong links between Minoan and Mycenaean civilisation, and the decipherment of the script in the 1950s established that their common language was an archaic form of Greek. The extant tablets record accounts and inventories that have to do with the routine administration of the royal palaces. How widely the script was known and used cannot be ascertained. There is no evidence that it was used to record literature. The script is, comparatively speaking, a cumbersome one, and could hardly have been used for a literary work of the length of the *Odyssey*, even supposing that suitable materials were available, such as leather or parchment. Nevertheless the existence of the script is an indication of the developed material culture of Mycenaean Greece.

After the destruction of Cnossus in 1400BC, Mycenaean civilisation was at its most powerful and advanced. The most substantial remains at Mycenae, the so-called Treasury of Atreus and the Tomb of Clytemnestra (Atreus was the father of Agamemnon and Clytemnestra was Agamemnon's wife) were built after 1300BC and the Lion Gate of Mycenae (so called from the relief over its lintel) dates from 1250BC. The fortification walls were mighty indeed. They were between twelve to forty-five feet thick and it has been estimated that they were as high as forty feet. The treasures found by Schliemann in the royal graves at Mycenae which include the famous gold face masks, bear witness to the opulent beauty of Mycenaean art work which was highly sophisticated in its craftsmanship and design. The techniques of engraving, enchasing and embossing were well developed and so was the art of inlaying bronze with precious metals. Ivory and amber imported from the east and the north are commonly found and indicate the extent of Mycenaean commercial relations. Mycenaean pottery of this period is found widely throughout the Mediterranean, a further indication that the Mycenaeans were great sailors and traders.

Excavations at Hissarlik, the site of Troy, have revealed nine settlements, the sixth settlement having substantial fortifications and monumental walls. The seventh of these settlements was destroyed in a great fire in the mid-thirteenth century BC, so that archaeological evidence seems to support the possibility of an historical Trojan War of which the Homeric account records the poetic memory. Soon after this possible date for the fall of Troy, Mycenaean power began to decline until

in about 1120BC Mycenae and Tiryns and with them the Mycenaean
culture of the Bronze Age were destroyed by the Dorians invading
from the west. The Dorians were themselves Greek speaking and pos-
sibly lived on the fringe of the Mycenaean empire. They initiated what
is usually known as the Dark Ages, lasting from 1100 to 800BC. The
Bronze Age gave way to the new Age of Iron. Refugees from the dis-
persal on mainland Greece created by the Dorian invasion now began
to colonise the eastern seaboard of the Aegean Sea known as Ionia in
Asia Minor. The Homeric poems are generally considered to have been
composed in Ionia (largely on linguistic grounds); they may therefore
preserve the memory of the Mycenaean mother culture transmitted by
those who had colonised Asia Minor.

The language of Homer

Historians of the Greek language have identified the same kind of
layered structure as that revealed by the archaeologists in which archaic
elements exist side by side with later Ionic forms. The language of
Homer is a fusion of elements from various dialects the chief of which
are the Ionic, the Aeolic, and the Arcadian. The predominant element
is the Ionic, and this is the main reason for believing that the Homeric
poems emanate from Ionia, but the Arcadian and Aeolic forms and
vocabulary suggest that the Homeric epic has its roots in earlier times.
The Arcadian and Aeolic dialects are descendants of dialects of Greek
spoken in mainland Greece in the south and north respectively during
the Mycenaean period. The fusion of these dialects with the Ionic has
resulted in the view that Ionic bards took over and adapted to new cir-
cumstances and a new audience material that they had inherited from
the past.

It is not simply a question of the fusion of different dialect forms
and vocabulary which suggests that the language of the Homeric
poems has a long and complicated history. Study of Homeric composi-
tion has revealed a highly sophisticated process at work which can only
have been refined over a long period of time. The process involves the
development and use of formulae, the stock in trade of the oral poet
who composed without the aid of writing. Some recurring Homeric
formulae have become world famous such as 'the wine-dark sea', 'rosy-
fingered dawn' or 'winged words'. Formulae may be short phrases like
the above or extend to longer passages describing oft repeated actions
such as putting out to sea, the preparation of a meal or the ritual of
sacrifice. Formulae are convenient units that can be readily committed
to memory and are therefore an aid to improvisation for the oral poet
who is wholly dependant upon memory. In a famous study of Homeric
formulae in the 1920s the American Homeric scholar Milman Parry

(1902–1935) demonstrated both the scope and economy of the system of formulaic composition.

It is necessary to have some rudimentary knowledge of Greek metre and the structure of the Greek language to understand how the formulaic system works. Homer's metre is the hexameter, a metre of six units (called feet); it is an arrangement of long and short syllables according to fixed rules. A long syllable followed by two short ones is called a dactyl (hence Homer's metre is often known as the dactylic hexameter) and two long syllables together are called a spondee. The scansion is as follows:

$$ - \cup \cup \mid - \cup \cup \mid - \cup \cup \mid - \cup \cup \mid - \cup \cup \mid - - $$
$$ - - - - - - - -   - \cup $$

The first four feet may be either dactyls or spondees (with usually more dactyls than spondees). The fifth must be a dactyl and the final foot is never a dactyl but the final syllable may be short, thus making a trochee. Greek metre is quantitative, that is, words are fitted into the metrical pattern according to length of syllable. (In English metre the pattern is determined by accent, by the stress given words in pronunciation.) Greek is an inflected language so that the forms of nouns and adjectives change according to the particular case in question, whether nominative, vocative, accusative, genitive or dative.

Homer has a number of adjectives to describe the hero of the *Odyssey*. All of these adjectives are generally appropriate to his character and role. But what Parry demonstrated is that in any particular context what governs the choice of a particular adjective is above all a metrical consideration. The various noun/adjective combinations (and sometimes there can be more than one adjective) all make different metrical patterns so that they can be slotted into the metre in different places. There are many combinations of noun and adjective for Odysseus. Each of these is determined by the case of the noun and by the position that the noun has in the verse, but no one of these combinations duplicates another; they are all metrically different. The scope is evident in the large number of combinations which have been developed to meet any syntactical and metrical need. The economy is evident in the fact that each of these combinations is unique, metrically speaking, and therefore allows the poet great flexibility in expression. Metre, of course, in any poetry determines what can and what cannot be said. What is remarkable about Parry's analysis of Homeric composition is that it suggests the restrictions inherent in oral composition and the extraordinary technical virtuosity through which they have been overcome.

The formulaic character of Homeric epic can explain how it is that there are various layers, the earliest of which transmit relics of Mycenaean times. The oldest linguistic elements are probably what have come to be known as the 'traditional epithets', such as 'owl-eyed Athene', 'cloud-gathering Zeus' or 'Triton-born Athene' some of which perplexed the Greeks themselves. The first systematic study of Homer in the late sixth century seems to have been concerned with the need to explain obsolete and difficult words. The formulaic character also explains why Homer's adjectives occasionally seem inappropriate in their particular context, why, for example, Penelope's hand is described as being thick (XXI, 6). Finally, the formulaic character of the epic goes some way to explain the obvious fact of repetition. About one third of the lines in the *Odyssey* are repeated wholly or in part in the course of the poem. Equally one third is not made up of phrases found elsewhere. It is clear that the traditional inheritance was constantly being added to and varied to meet contemporary needs and the requirements of different tales. Homer's language, therefore, had been purposely developed for poetic recitation; it was never a spoken language. Nor did such a development, any more than the myths or the tales themselves, originate with one genius. There is a consensus of scholarly opinion that the language of the Homeric poems evolved over many centuries and that its technique of formulaic diction goes back to the Mycenaean age from which it was no doubt transmitted by practising bards like Demodocus and Phemius in the *Odyssey*.

Some problems

Here the consensus stops and the Homeric Question remains. The poetic excellence of the Homeric poems presupposes individual talent. Nobody can believe that the lost tradition consists of countless poems of the quality of the *Odyssey* and *Iliad* which have not come down to us. Where does the individual talent stand in relation to the tradition? Most would say that 'Homer' came at the end of it. But was he a fully oral poet like Demodocus and Phemius, or did he use the oral method simply because he was composing for recitation? Did he dictate the text to a scribe, or did he write it himself? These are all open questions.

Comparisons with oral epics in other cultures show that in pre-literate cultures feats of memory that would be considered to be astonishing in a literate culture are common enough. Bards have recited from memory, or have improvised poems, that are longer than the *Odyssey*. But such poems are comparatively crude and do not have either the complex structure or the finished artistry of the Homeric poems. The difference in quality between the Homeric poems and oral epics in other cultures is more significant than anything that they have in common.

The problem is not made any easier by the inconclusive results of attempts to provide a date for the poems. The various layers that are apparent in the *Odyssey* have been so fused that neither linguists nor archaeologists have been able to unravel the puzzle. Most authorities envisage a date somewhere in the eighth century BC for the composition of the poems.

Nor is it known for certain when writing was introduced in Greece. Evidence suggests that knowledge and use of the syllabic Linear B script referred to earlier did not survive the fall of Mycenaean civilisation in the late twelfth century BC. Sometime between the tenth century and the eighth a new alphabetic script from Phoenicia was adopted in Greece. Papyrus (a form of paper originating in Egypt) seems not to have been introduced until later. Leather is known to have been used for writing quite early, though it would have been a costly business to commit a poem the size of the *Odyssey* to leather. Any kind of book is a rarity until the fifth century BC. Nevertheless the materials were available and it is theoretically possible that the poems were committed to writing at an early stage.

The history of the written text

The earliest written text of Homer for which there is any evidence in Greek sources dates from the late sixth century BC when the Athenian leader of the day is reported to have brought texts of the poems to Athens and to have required the rhapsodes who recited Homer's poetry at the annual Athenian festival to do so one after another in proper order so that the poem would be recited as a whole. Given the special status of Homer in Greek culture from the earliest times, attested in the formation of special guilds of rhapsodes to recite the poems, it is certainly credible that there was a need for a definitive text.

The first textual criticism of Homer was carried out in the third and second centuries BC at Alexandria in the famous library there by a succession of scholars, the most notable of whom was Aristarchus (*c.* 215–145BC). Many texts of Homer had been collected for the Alexandrian library, and divergencies in the number of lines and variations in wording were glaringly apparent. At this time the Homeric text was standardised, and each poem was split up into twenty-four books, each given a letter of the Greek alphabet and a title heading still used to this day. This text standardised at Alexandria is the ancestor of all the texts that have come down to the modern world.

The Alexandrian version was copied, like other ancient texts, on papyrus rolls until the late second century AD when the codex (a book with pages) was introduced and papyrus was gradually replaced by the more durable parchment. The oldest surviving complete manuscripts are medieval, but fragments of the poems on papyrus survive from Graeco-Roman times. Some manuscripts preserve the opinions of the ancient commentators and the notes of Alexandrian textual critics in the form of scholia, comments written in the margins above and beside the text. Similar material is also incorporated in compilations made by Byzantine scholars from collections of material now lost. The most notable of these compilations is the vast commentary on the poems made sometime in the twelfth century by Eustathius, Archbishop of Thessalonika. These Byzantine commentaries, the scholia and ancient papyri have all been used by modern textual critics to arrive at the best possible text of the Homeric poems.

There have been many editions of the *Odyssey* since the first edition printed in Florence in 1488. A reliable plain text of the Greek is the Oxford Classical Text of the *Odyssey* edited by T.W. Allen in two volumes published by the Clarendon Press, Oxford in 1917. An informative edition for students is *The Odyssey of Homer* edited with general and grammatical introduction, commentary and indexes by W.B. Stanford in two volumes published by Macmillan, London, in 1948–50.

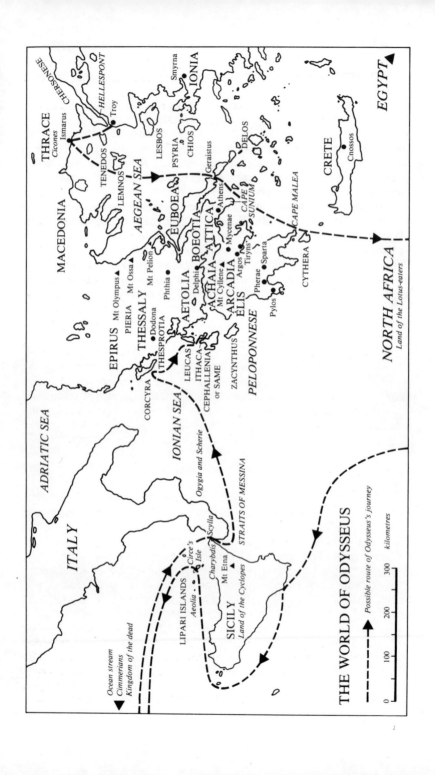

THE WORLD OF ODYSSEUS

– – – Possible route of Odysseus's journey

| 0 | 100 | 200 | 300 | kilometres |

Part 2

Summaries

of the ODYSSEY

THE NOTES THAT FOLLOW the summaries are designed to elucidate mythical and geographical references and to explain Greek antiquities. They deal with matters of substance rather than expression and can therefore be used with any reasonably close translation.

The words in heavy type are either a literal version of what is in Homer such as 'the oxen of Hyperion' in the opening lines or a summary version such as 'Odysseus like a lion' referring to a whole simile in Book IV. Sometimes the words in heavy type allude to longer passages like 'Athene tells Telemachus her tale' at the end of Book I, or isolate a theme or motif such as 'death at sea' about which a general point is being made.

Most of the words explained or commented upon are proper names. Persons and places are given their Greek names even where they are more familiarly known in their Roman form, for example, Heracles rather than Hercules, and Odysseus rather than Ulysses (probably derived from an Aeolic form of the Greek). An exception is made in Part 3 in quotations where Roman forms such as Ulysses or Jupiter and Juno (for Zeus and Hera) are used by the author of the quotation or translation. Greek names are given in the form in which they are most familiar in English: Achilles, for example, rather than Akilleus, Ajax not Aias and Ithaca not Ithaka.

Most of the place names can be found on the map provided though it should be remembered that identification of place names in Homer is often dubious and frequently a matter of scholarly dispute. Many of the places visited by Odysseus are imaginary and Homer does not always suggest their location in relation to known landmarks so that it is not really possible to pinpoint Odysseus's journey on an actual map.

The bracketed title headings are translations of the Greek titles given to individual books by the Greeks, when the Homeric poems were first edited by Alexandrian scholars in the second century BC.

Some cross-references are given to elucidate the structure of the poem or to suggest a recurring theme. These references are to the Greek text and can therefore be looked up in any numbered modern text. The bilingual Loeb edition has the numbered Greek text with a translation on the facing page. Most translations also give Homer's line numbers. In the Penguin edition they are to be found at the top of each page.

A general summary

The poet introduces the saga of Odysseus, the hero who went with the Greeks to Troy and after the ten years siege was destined to undertake a great journey on which he saw many peoples and had many adventures, in the course of which all his companions perished. The muse begins the tale at the time, just before his final return home to the island of Ithaca, when Odysseus, who has been a prisoner of the nymph Calypso for seven years on the island of Ogygia, is about to be released. In a council of the gods in the absence of Poseidon, who is hostile to Odysseus because he has blinded his son Polyphemus the Cyclops, Athene protests on behalf of her favourite Odysseus and Zeus agrees to send Hermes to order Calypso to allow him to go home. She proposes to go to Ithaca herself in order to prompt Telemachus, the son of Odysseus, first to call an assembly to denounce the suitors who are occupying his house and wasting his property while they woo his mother Penelope, and second, to make a journey to Pylos and Sparta in search of news of his father from his old comrades who have returned from Troy, Nestor and Menelaus. This is the subject of Books I–IV sometimes called the Telemachid or the Telemacheia.

In the disguise of a stranger, Athene is welcomed by Telemachus who explains to her the situation in the palace. His mother is trying to ward off the advances of the suitors in loyalty to Odysseus. Athene gives her advice. Telemachus asserts himself in dealing with his mother and in proposing an assembly of all the Ithacans for the following day (Book I).

In the assembly Telemachus denounces the suitors but they show no intention of leaving, complaining of Penelope's behaviour and advising him to send her back to her father's house. Telemachus asks for a ship to make his journey. In the palace that night they mock Telemachus but he nevertheless manages to acquire his ship and sets off for Pylos (Book II). Here he meet Nestor and hears of his father's exploits at Troy and of the return of other Greek heroes from the Trojan campaign. But Nestor knows nothing of Odysseus's present whereabouts (Book III). Telemachus journeys on to Sparta where he is entertained by Menelaus and Helen who also have reminiscences of his father and the returning Greeks. Menelaus tells of the news he received from the divine prophet Proteus that Odysseus is a prisoner on Calypso's island. Back in Ithaca the suitors plot to kill Telemachus in an ambush on his return (Book IV).

In a second council of the gods Zeus sends Hermes to tell Calypso to release Odysseus. Odysseus builds a raft and sets sail for Scherie, a journey of twenty days. On the eighteenth day Poseidon, on his return from a visit to the Ethiopians, catches sight of Odysseus, and raises a storm in which he is shipwrecked. Eventually after great difficulty and peril he lands in Scherie (Book V).

After a night's rest he is awakened by the sound of female voices and encounters Nausicaa the daughter of King Alcinous of the Phaeacians, who, together with her maids, is washing clothes in an adjacent river. She directs him to the palace and recommends that he petition her mother Queen Arete (Book VI). This he does, asking for passage home. In response to Arete's enquiry he tells of his stay with Calypso and his journey from Ogygia (Book VII). The following day he is entertained by the Phaeacians. There is dancing and song from the bard Demodocus. Games are held in which Odysseus distinguishes himself when provoked into competition by an insult from a young Phaeacian. At the evening banquet Demodocus sings of the Wooden Horse. Noting his tearful reaction Alcinous asks Odysseus to give an account of himself (Book VIII).

In reply Odysseus tells of his wanderings from Troy before he reached Calypso's island in a narrative that extends over four books (IX–XII) called by the ancients 'narratives to Alcinous'. He begins with the sack of Ismarus and the encounter with the Cicones, followed by encounters with the Lotus-eaters and with the Cyclops (Book IX). He then meets Aeolus, the Laestrygonians and Circe who tells him that he must consult Tiresias in Hades (Book X). Following Circe's instructions he summons up the spirits of the dead and speaks first with Tiresias who tells him not to harm the oxen of the Sun, informs him of trouble at home and prophesies his future, and then Odysseus speaks to his mother Anticleia. There follows the catalogue of famous women. Odysseus then speaks with Agamemnon, Achilles and Ajax, and sees other heroes (Book XI). Circe, to whom he then returns, tells him of dangers to come. He avoids the Wandering Rocks but encounters the Sirens and then Scylla and Charybdis. Finally he reaches Thrinacie where his men kill the oxen of the Sun. They lose their lives when Zeus wrecks their ship with a thunderbolt. Odysseus, the sole survivor, drifts to the island of Ogygia (Book XII).

The Phaeacians escort Odysseus loaded with gifts in one of their magic ships by night to Ithaca. When he wakes up on the Ithacan shore where he had been left asleep he does not recognise the place. Athene in disguise enlightens him. Disguising his own identity Odysseus tells his first Cretan tale. The goddess reveals herself, plans his disguise as a beggar and sets him on the road to the dwelling of Eumaeus his loyal steward (Book XIII). Eumaeus welcomes the stranger, who tells his second Cretan tale to conceal his identity (Book XIV). Telemachus makes hasty preparations to return home. Odysseus enquires about his father Laertes. Eumaeus tells his own history. Telemachus lands in Ithaca, having evaded the plot of the suitors (Book XV). He arrives at

Eumaeus's hut. Odysseus reveals himself to his son and together they plot the destruction of the suitors. The suitors, realising that Telemachus has escaped, discuss a further plot to ambush him on his return to the palace (Book XVI).

The action now moves to the palace. Telemachus sets off first, followed later by Odysseus and Eumaeus. En route Odysseus is insulted by the goatherd Melantheus. He enters the palace and begs from the suitors. Antinous their leader throws a stool at him (Book XVII). He fights with the beggar Irus and is insulted by a maidservant Melantho and by another suitor Eurymachus (Book XVIII). He speaks with Penelope and repeats his Cretan history to her. He is washed by his old nurse Eurycleia who recognises him from his scar. She is sworn to secrecy. Penelope announces to the stranger her decision to institute the contest with the bow with the intention of marrying the winner (Book XIX). Odysseus sees the waste of his resources in the preparations being made for a banquet. He is insulted by the suitor Ctesippus. The prophet Theoclymenus foresees the suitors' doom (Book XX). Penelope fetches the bow which the suitors try but fail to string. Odysseus asks if he may try his hand. Telemachus orders that he be given the bow which he successfully strings, shooting through the twelve axes (Book XXI).

Now begins the killing of the suitors and the re-establishment of Odysseus as master of his own house. Antinous falls first. Odysseus then reveals himself and so commences the general slaughter. The errant maids are hanged and the house fumigated (Book XXII). Eurycleia gives the news to Penelope who cannot believe that her husband has returned. After testing him she eventually suspends her disbelief and Odysseus tells her of his wanderings (Book XXIII). The souls of the suitors are ushered by Hermes into Hades where the spirit of Agamemnon asks them what has happened to bring so many of them at once. When Amphimedon tells him, Agamemnon extols Odysseus's action and Penelope's virtue. Odysseus goes to his father's farm for the final recognition scene. The relatives of the suitors, in an assembly, decide to avenge the death of their sons. Laertes, Odysseus and Telemachus commence battle which is stopped by Zeus and Athene who command the peace with which the poem ends (Book XXIV).

Detailed summaries

Book I (The Assembly of the Gods.
The Exhortation of Athene to Telemachus)

See the opening paragraphs of the general summary for a summary of this book.

NOTES AND GLOSSARY:

the Muse: the goddess of poetry. According to later writers there were nine Muses who were the daughters of Zeus and Memory, each presiding over one of the major arts (see also XXIV, 60)

Troy: the siege of Troy (in Asia Minor), undertaken after the Trojan Paris had abducted the Greek Helen from Sparta, had lasted ten years. The stratagem of the Wooden Horse by which Troy was finally taken was devised by Odysseus (see VIII, 492–520). Menelaus, the husband of Helen, describes Odysseus's crucial role in restraining the Greeks inside the horse from shouting out and revealing their presence (IV, 266–89)

the oxen of Hyperion: the episode is narrated by Odysseus to the Phaeacians (XII, 265–375). Hyperion is another name for Helios the sun-god in Homer

the nymph Calypso: the daughter of Atlas, the Titan (a son of Heaven and Earth) who supported the world. The word nymph indicates that she was a minor deity to be distinguished from the major deities who dwelt on Mount Olympus

Ithaca: Odysseus's island home off north-west Greece. Its precise identification is a matter of dispute

Poseidon: the god of the sea, and brother of Zeus and Hades. One of his epithets is 'girdler of the earth' presumably from the Homeric belief that the earth is surrounded by Ocean stream. He is also responsible for earthquakes and so is called the earthshaker. The emblem of his power is the trident, a three-pronged spear. One of the most powerful Olympians who hates Odysseus because he has blinded his son Polyphemus the Cyclops (see lines 68–71)

Ethiopians: from the Homeric point of view they were a remote people living at the edge of the world

Olympian Zeus: the son of Cronos, whose rule he overthrew, and parent of many of the other gods. He is the most powerful of the Olympians, often referred to as their king, and his special province is the upper air where he controls storms and clouds and sends rain. His power is expressed in his thunderbolt (see XII, 405–17). He thunders to encourage Odysseus at XX, 102–19. Another of his emblems is the eagle. There is a famous description of Olympus, a

	mountain in northern Greece and the home of the gods, at VI, 43–5
Agamemnon:	son of Atreus and brother of Menelaus, the husband of Helen. Leader of the Greek expeditions against Troy he was killed on his return by his wife Clytemnestra and her paramour Aegisthus
Hermes:	the messenger of the gods. On the orders of Zeus (his father) he killed Argus, a monster with a hundred eyes, whom Hera (the wife of Zeus) had ordered to watch over Io, a beautiful young woman transformed into a cow by Zeus to cover up his amour with her
Athene:	the virgin warrior goddess, daughter of Zeus and champion of Odysseus. She is also the goddess of wisdom
Argives:	literally natives of Argos. Argos in Homeric usage often means simply the Greek mainland south of the isthmus of Corinth, so that Argives are Greeks. They are also known as Achaeans and Danaans
Taphian:	the Taphians were pirates and sea traders living north of Ithaca (see XVI, 424–30)
Telemachus:	the name means far fighter. He gives Athene the welcome traditional for guests and strangers. The Greek for stranger is *zeinos* whence zenophobia. A great ethical imperative in the *Odyssey* is zenophilia (the offering of hospitality to strangers)
Phemius:	the name means praiser, he who gives fame. Note that he is not willingly a party to the suitors' behaviour
Athene tells Telemachus her tale:	the first of many traveller's tales. She claims that her family and that of Telemachus are guest friends, that is, families who have exchanged hospitality and so have claims upon one another
an augur:	one who tells the future, usually by observing the behaviour of birds, a prophet
death at sea:	Odysseus fearing death by drowning similarly laments that he could not have died heroically at Troy (see V, 299–312)
Dulichium, Same and Zacynthus:	neighbouring islands. There are over one hundred suitors (see XVI, 245–51)
Penelope's father:	Icarius, a Spartan and brother of Tyndareus, father of Helen. In Homeric times a wife could not inherit property in her own right. It seems here the suitors are required to give gifts to the bride's father

Nestor: the oldest of the Greeks at Troy, famous for his advice and tactical skill. He is somewhat garrulous
Menelaus: now reunited with Helen with whom he lives in tranquil amity. All is forgiven (see IV)
Telemachus no longer a child: his coming of age sets the plot in motion
gifts for the departing guest: a feature of Homeric hospitality (see, XV, 80−5)
the kingship of Ithaca: this does not necessarily come to the head of Odysseus's house. Telemachus claims merely his father's house and property as his patrimony
Antinous: the name suggests one who is antagonistic. The suitors, like Penelope, are surprised at Telemachus's boldness
the tunic: a close-fitting shift made of linen which reached below the knees. A large woollen cloak thrown over the shoulders was worn out of doors

---

Book II (The Ithacan Assembly. The Journey of Telemachus)

In the assembly of the Ithacans Telemachus denounces the behaviour of the suitors. Their leader Antinous in reply puts the blame on Penelope for delaying and not making up her mind. He advises Telemachus to send his mother to her father's house so that a new marriage can be arranged. An omen is interpreted by a soothsayer as portending the return of Odysseus and a battle with the suitors. Eurymachus angrily dismisses the soothsayer, reiterating Antinous's advice to Telemachus. Telemachus then requests a ship to make his journey to find definite news of his father. Athene encourages Telemachus in his projected journey. Preparations are made and he sets out at night.

NOTES AND GLOSSARY:
the assembly of all the people: held in the market place. The Greek word *agora* means market place, council and assembly. This is the ancestor of the assembly that was the cornerstone of the Athenian democracy. Here the assembly has no effective power
the Cyclops: Odysseus tells his story in IX
Ilium: another name for Troy, from Ilus, according to some accounts the founder of the city
Peisenor: means man persuader, an appropriate name for a herald
Telemachus accuses the suitors: he argues that the people of Ithaca should feel outrage and shame at their behaviour. (Most of the suitors are from neighbouring islands.) Their conduct shows no sense of shame.

The Greek word *aidos* means a restraining sense of shame, self respect, honour

Themis: the personification of the order of things established by law, custom and equity, so that she is described as the convener of assemblies here

Telemachus's tears: show his inexperience

Athene: also presides over the mechanical arts such as spinning and weaving

Tyro: beloved of Poseidon from whom Nestor and Jason the Argonaut were descended (see XI, 235)

Alcmene: beloved of Zeus by whom she bore Heracles (see XI, 266)

Mycene: a daughter of Inarchus, a river god of the Argive plain, who gave her name to Mycenae

the Furies: they avenge offences in the family; the Furies pursue Orestes after he has killed his mother Clytemnestra

the nemesis of men: Telemachus fears the just indignation of public opinion if he were to send Penelope back to Icarius

eagles: the birds of Zeus

Haliserthes Mastorides: means sea bold, son of seeker, appropriate for a fearless soothsayer

nineteen years: ten years at Troy and nine years returning

Mentor: his name has become proverbial for a guide or protector. He makes it clear that the suitors are a small minority when compared with numbers at the Ithacan assembly

Athene condemns the suitors: they have neither understanding nor a sense of what is right (*dike*)

Telemachus rebukes Antinous: he was just a child when the suitors first came; now that he has grown up things will be different

Ephyre: Athene had told of Odysseus's journey to Ephyre in search of poison to smear on his arrows (I, 257–64)

Book III (At Pylos)

Telemachus arrives at Pylos where he finds Nestor and his sons sacrificing to Poseidon on the shore. Nestor welcomes him, reminisces about Odysseus, tells of the fate of the returning Greeks and offers advice to Telemachus. He stays overnight with Nestor, and, after a morning sacrifice, sets off for Sparta to see Menelaus, accompanied by Nestor's son Peisistratus.

NOTES AND GLOSSARY:

Neleus: the father of Nestor who according to some accounts built the royal palace at Pylos

the sacrifice: the thighs wrapped in fat and soaked in wine were offered to the gods. Bulls are associated with Poseidon elsewhere

Peisistratus: means persuader of the army; doubtless he was so named from the persuasive powers of his father Nestor

aegis-bearing Zeus: the aegis, literally a storm cloud, is a heavy shield with a hundred golden tassels, the means of raising tempests and creating panic among mortals

Athene is pleased with Peisistratus: she calls him *dikaios*. Note how she had earlier dismissed the suitors for lacking *dike*

Gerenian Nestor: so called because he had been among the Gerenians when Heracles invaded Pylos and killed all his brothers

Amphitrite: a sea goddess; or simply the sea

Achilles: the strong man of the Greeks whose anger is the subject of the *Iliad*

Priam: the old king of Troy, father of Hector and Paris

Ajax: a stout man in defence, second only to Achilles in fighting power. After the death of Achilles, killed by an arrow in his heel from Paris, there was a dispute as to who should receive his famous armour which had been made by the god Hephaestus. It was claimed by both Odysseus and Ajax, and went to Odysseus. Ajax planned a night attack on his own allies but Athene drove him mad with the result that he killed a flock of sheep instead. When he came to his senses, he committed suicide in shame

Patroclus: the comrade of Achilles whose death in the sixteenth book is the pivotal action of the *Iliad*

Antilochus: killed by Memnon, son of the dawn goddess Aurora. He takes part in the chariot race in the funeral games in honour of Patroclus

the anger of Athene: one of the Greeks had raped Cassandra the prophetic daughter of Priam in the temple of Athene. The Greeks failed to punish the offender so that Athene prevailed upon Poseidon to raise a storm which scattered the returning fleet

the sons of Atreus: Agamemnon and Menelaus

Tenedos: an island off the Trojan coast

Diomedes:	another of the famous Greek fighters at Troy. In *Iliad* V he even wounds the gods
Lesbos:	all these places can be identified on the map provided
Achilles's son:	is Pyrrhus and is also called Neoptolemus. The Myrmidons are the followers of Achilles and Pyrrhus
Philoctetes:	the dying Heracles gave him his bow and arrows which were an indispensible part of Troy's downfall
Idomeneus:	his exploits feature in *Iliad* XIII
Orestes:	compare Athene's exhortation at I, 298–302. The lines are repeated here
Sunium:	on the south-east of Attica of which region Athens is the capital
Phoebus Apollo:	the sun god; *phoebos* means bright. He is also an archer
Malea:	the most easterly of the three large promontories of the Peloponnese
Lacedaemon:	another name for Sparta
the Caucones:	a tribe living not far from Pylos
Triton-born Athene:	many of Homer's epithets are of uncertain meaning
′ Hades:	the name both of a god (the brother of Zeus and Poseidon) and of the underworld over which he was king and where resided the spirits of the dead
Polycaste bathes Telemachus:	women regularly wash men in the Homeric poems
Pherae:	probably in Arcadia, halfway between Pylos and Sparta

---

Book IV (At Sparta)

Arriving at Sparta, Telemachus is welcomed by Menelaus and Helen who grieve over the past and tell of their memories of Odysseus including the story of the Wooden Horse. On the following day Telemachus asks for news of his father. Menelaus tells of his own homecoming and how he met Proteus in Egypt who told him of the homecoming of other Greek leaders including Odysseus. Telemachus is prevailed upon to stay at Sparta. Back in Ithaca the suitors plot to ambush him on his return. Penelope hears about it but is comforted in a dream sent by Athene.

NOTES AND GLOSSARY:
golden Aphrodite: the goddess of love and beauty

Cyprus to Libya: Menelaus travelled from east to west throughout the Mediterranean in seven years amassing a fortune though Homer does not say by what means

Artemis: sister of Apollo, the beautiful goddess of chastity. Helen's wifely domestication is apparent in the emphasis on her spinning

the basket on wheels: Mycenaean craftmanship was highly sophisticated

the anodyne: Egyptian medicine had been highly developed

Paeeon: the word means healer in Greek

Odysseus in disguise as a beggar: prefiguring the later disguise

Helen repents: saying she was the victim of infatuation

Deiphobus: after Hector was killed by Achilles, Deiphobus became leader of the Trojans, and after the death of Paris he married Helen

Odysseus like a lion: the first extended simile in the *Odyssey*

Philomeleides: the name suggests a lover of limbs, that is, someone who cultivates physical fitness appropriate for a wrestler

Menelaus and Proteus: a typically Odyssean adventure

Ajax: not the Ajax who quarrelled with Odysseus but the son of Oileus. His boast shows him to be guilty of hubris, arrogant behaviour that offends the gods

Hera: the wife (and sister) of Zeus and queen of heaven. She supported the Greek cause at Troy and is prominent in the *Iliad*. She has little to do in the *Odyssey*

Thyestes: brother of Atreus which means that Aegisthus and Agamemnon are cousins

the Elysian plain: the Homeric paradise

Rhadamanthus: a son of Zeus and brother of King Minos of Crete. Because of his uprightness in life he was made a judge of the underworld after his death and took up his abode in Elysium

the king of Sidon: a rich city famous for craftsmen

Book V (The Cave of Calypso. The Raft of Odysseus)

Zeus sends Hermes to order Calypso to let Odysseus return home. She is reluctant, but tells Odysseus to make preparations. He builds a raft and sets sail. As he comes in sight of Scherie, Poseidon wrecks his boat in a storm. Only after great difficulty and peril does he make land.

NOTES AND GLOSSARY:

Tithonus: he fell in love with the dawn and prayed for immortality so that he could love her always. This the gods granted to him, but they did not give him immortal youth, so that he lived eternally in ever increasing decrepitude

Pieria: a mountainous district in Macedonia in northern Greece

Ogygia: usually thought to be fictional

Calypso's cave: a famous description

Orion: a giant hunter who became a constellation

Demeter: goddess of the earth

Calypso's oath: the gods are not to be trusted unless they swear an oath. The most solemn oath is by Styx, the river of the underworld of death

ambrosia: the word means immortal, and is used for the food eaten by the immortals

Pleiads and Bootes: the latter is the ploughman. The Great Bear is still visible in the sky after the other stars have set

the Solymi: a people in or near Lycia in Asia Minor

Odysseus's lament: shows his heroic spirit in wishing for a death that would have made him famous

Ino: an insignificant minor deity only mentioned here. Leucothoe means white goddess

Aegae: an island off Euboea

Book VI (The Coming of Odysseus to the Phaeacians)

Nausicaa, daughter of Alcinous king of the Phaeacians, is prompted by Athene to go with her maids to wash clothes in a nearby river. Here Odysseus is awakened by their cries as they play a game with a ball. He approaches Nausicaa and asks for help which she willingly gives in the form of food, clothing and directions to the palace. She advises him to supplicate her mother Queen Arete. Odysseus travels to the palace after her to avoid scandal and reaches the city.

NOTES AND GLOSSARY:

the Phaeacians: Zeus refers to them as kinsmen of the gods (V, 35). Scherie is probably imaginary. Some have identified it with Corcyra (now Corfu)

the Cyclopes: individuals without the social bond; they are sharply contrasted with the Phaeacians

Alcinous: his name suggests strength of mind

Leto: mother of the twins Artemis and Apollo by Zeus. Taygetus and Erymanthus are mountains in the Peloponnese. Artemis is the goddess of chastity and also of hunting and is closely associated with the natural world

the nymphs:	in Greek myth there are indwelling spirits in all natural things
clasp the knees:	a usual mode of supplication in Greek culture
Delos:	a small island in the Aegean on which Apollo and Artemis were born. A sacred place
Hephaestus:	the god of metalwork; the divine artificer
her father's brother:	Poseidon

Book VII (Odysseus's Approach to Alcinous)

The palace and gardens of Alcinous are described. Odysseus enters, and petitions Arete for help and passage home. He is given food and drink, and promised the desired passage home. In answer to Arete's questioning he tells of his journey from Ogygia to Scherie.

NOTES AND GLOSSARY:

Eurymedusa:	means wide-ruling, a dignified name
Arete:	the name means she who is prayed for or to
Eurymedon:	Arete and Alcinous are of divine descent
Marathon:	on the coast of Attica, twenty-six miles from Athens
Erechtheus:	legendary king of Athens. The Erechtheum on the Acropolis is named after him
the palace:	a magnificent building (compare the palace of Menelaus IV, 43–51)
the formal garden:	this might be contrasted with the wildness of Calypso's cave
the spinners:	the Fates. Later writers distinguished three, Clotho who spins the wool, Lachesis who measures and allots the thread, and Atropos who cuts it
further than Euboea:	this implies that Scherie is to the west of the Greek mainland
Tityos:	a giant who lived in Euboea. He attempted to rape Leto and was cast into Tartarus, the place of punishment in Hades, where a vulture devoured his liver. Nothing is known about the visit to him of Rhadamanthus (see XI, 576–81). The allusion, like the excursus on the ancestry of the king and queen, serves to enhance the Phaeacians by association with characters famous in old myth and legend

---

Book VIII (The Introduction of Odysseus to the Phaeacians)

In the Phaeacian assembly it is agreed to send Odysseus home by ship. Alcinous proposes to entertain his guest and the Phaeacians. There is a

banquet in the palace after which the blind bard Demodocus sings.
Games follow. Odysseus is provoked into competing by the insult of a
young Phaeacian. He distinguishes himself with the discus. Demodo-
cus sings of the love of Ares and Aphrodite. Dancing follows. Odys-
seus receives gifts from his hosts. After supper Demodocus sings of the
Wooden Horse. Odysseus's tearful response is noted by Alcinous who
asks him to give an account of himself.

NOTES AND GLOSSARY:
Demodocus: means esteemed by the people
deeds of fame: Achilles consoles himself by singing of the deeds of famous men at *Iliad* IX, 186
the quarrel of Odysseus and Achilles: not referred to elsewhere in Homer. Ancient commentators record that after the death of Hector the two quarrelled as to whether Troy could best be taken by force of arms or by a stratagem, Odysseus favouring the latter
Apollo: is also the god of prophecy. His most famous oracle was at Delphi in northern Greece, formerly known as Pytho after the dragon (python) killed there by Apollo. Oracles were delivered through the medium of priests who were inspired by the god, and were sought by military and political leaders throughout the Greek world over many centuries
Acroneos: means topship. All the names here have nautical associations, appropriate for a seafaring people
Ares: the god of war
fame through the games: note the desire for excellence, characteristic of Homeric man in sport as in the more serious aspects of life
Euryalus rebukes Odysseus: the heroic spirit despises trade and the pursuit of material gain. Menelaus, however, spends seven years amassing treasure and piracy seems to be almost an acceptable pastime in the *Odyssey*. There is perhaps some ambivalence here
the all-round man: Odysseus does in fact have all these desirable qualities. He is intelligent and eloquent while having strength and good looks (note the famous description of him at VI, 229–35). In this respect he represents the Greek ideal
Philoctetes: to whom Heracles gave his bow and arrows. Doubtless much is made of Odysseus's skill in archery here because of the role it will play in the final dénouement

Heracles and Eurytus: the former is a son of Zeus, famous for his twelve labours. The latter, according to some accounts, was Heracles's teacher in the art of bowmanship. Both were heroes of a previous generation

Phaeacian delights: as a result of these lines the Phaeacians have been regarded as over fond of soft and luxurious living. Yet they also boast of their prowess in sport and they are expert seamen. As for hot baths, Odysseus himself takes pleasure in one after the games (VIII, 450−2). Note too that Eurycleia prepares a hot bath for the stranger at XIX, 388 so that a hot bath may be regarded as a regular feature of civilised living. In the life of the Phaeacians there is a blend of the practical and the athletic with the aesthetic which is characteristically Greek

the stewards who prepare the hall: a further indication of the well-ordered society

the love of Ares and Aphrodite: a famous comic interlude which has been much censured on the grounds of its immorality though it could be argued that it is highly moral since adultery is made ridiculous and punished. The tale shows the triumph of craft and intelligence over passion and strength

Lemnos: the island on which Hephaestus fell when he was thrown from heaven (see *Iliad* I, 590−4)

Ares of the golden reins: Ares is frequently represented as riding furiously in his war chariot

Cytherea: Cythera is a Greek island sacred to Aphrodite because, according to some accounts, it was the place where she rose fully grown at her birth from the sea

Sintians: the inhabitants of Lemnos who rescued Hephaestus after he had been flung from heaven

father Zeus: Zeus is father of both Ares and Aphrodite and, according to some accounts, of Hephaestus too

the adulterer's fine: even a homicide could be expiated by money

Thrace: a wild region east of Macedonia always associated with Ares

the Graces: usually thought to be three in number

Apollo: the god not only of prophecy but also of poetry

Demodocus begins his song: 'taking it up at the place where', implying that the whole Trojan saga is now part of the bard's repertoire

Odysseus's tears: the Homeric heroes have no inhibition about dis-
plays of grief (compare Achilles at *Iliad* I, 348–63
and elsewhere)

Poseidon's anger: he is a morose and malevolent deity in the *Odyssey*.
He is the only god not to laugh at Ares and Aphro-
dite (line 344)

Book IX (Narratives to Alcinous. The Cyclops)

Odysseus reveals his identity and begins the narrative of his wanderings
after the fall of Troy with an account of the sack of Ismarus and his en-
counter with the Cicones. He and his men are blown from Cape Malea
to north Africa where they encounter the Lotus-eaters. They sail to
Sicily where they are imprisoned by the Cyclops in his cave. Odysseus
makes the Cyclops drunk, blinds him and then escapes, clinging to the
underside of the Cyclops's sheep as they are let out of the cave in
the morning.

NOTES AND GLOSSARY:

praise of the bard: a vivid evocation of a Homeric ideal (compare
XVII, 518–20)

Odysseus announces himself: pride in achievement and fame is char-
acteristic of the Homeric heroes

Aeaean: Aeaea is the island home of Circe

Ismarus: in Thrace, north-east of Troy. The Cicones were
allies of the Trojans

Malea: the most easterly of the three promontories of the
Peloponnese. Odysseus, therefore, was well on his
way home when he was blown off course

the Lotus-eaters: located on the north African coast, so that it is to
be inferred that Odysseus is blown right across the
Mediterranean due south of Greece by the north
wind

the land of the Cyclopes: identified as Sicily. Cyclops means round-
eyed. The Cyclopes are said to be *athemistes*
(having no regard for *themis*, custom, law or
equity). They do not practice agriculture, and live
each a law unto himself. This primitive state of
nature is in marked contrast to the civilised life of
the Phaeacians, once their neighbours. Odysseus's
description of their island's unrealised potential
serves to emphasise the achievement of the Phaea-
cians, and further suggests that Scherie is a desir-
able ideal fully approved of by Homer

Polyphemus's opening questions: these are a repetition of Nestor's questions at III, 71−4. In view of Odysseus's treatment of the Cicones, suspicion of the stranger is natural and justified. Nestor's questions, however, were put after he had fed his guests

the laws of hospitality: they are a fundamental feature of Homeric society and as central to the *Odyssey* as are the laws relating to treatment of the dead in the *Iliad*

Noman: a reminder that this tale is a very old one. Many versions of it exist in many cultures

Odysseus boasts: contrast XXII, 411−18 where Odysseus rebukes Eurycleia for boasting over the death of the suitors. Odysseus's triumph is of wit and intelligence over brute strength (compare the triumph of Hephaestus over Ares)

Book X (Aeolus. The Laestrygonians. Circe)

They sail on to Aeolia where Aeolus gives Odysseus a bag in which all the winds are imprisoned except the favourable west wind. His companions undo the bag with disastrous consequences. They come next to the land of the Laestrygonians, a race of cannibalistic giants. They escape to Aeaea where Circe turns Odysseus's men into swine. With the help of Hermes he masters Circe who then ceases to be hostile. He spends a year with the goddess. Before his departure Circe tells him that he must consult the spirit of the prophet Tiresias in Hades.

NOTES AND GLOSSARY:

Aeolia: north-west of Sicily identified by some with the Lipari islands

Aeolus: means changeful, an appropriate name for the ruler of the winds

Antiphates: his name suggests contradiction

Eurylochus: the only one of the companions of Odysseus who is individualised

the youthful Hermes: this is how he is represented in Greek culture

moly: probably imaginary. Circe's magic can be defeated only by magical means

his men like cows: many of Homer's similes are thematically appropriate. The comparison of men to animals is clever, given the earlier transformation

Eurylochus's rebuke: it is not without justice

Persephone: the daughter of Demeter and the wife of Hades; queen of the underworld

Tiresias: the most famous Greek prophet of a previous age
the river of Ocean: Ocean is imagined as a stream encircling the earth
(which is flat). It seems here that a descent into
Hades is not envisaged. Odysseus must simply
cross the Ocean stream. Elsewhere in Homer,
however, Hades does seem to be located under-
ground
Phlegethon, Cocytus, Styx and Acheron: they suggest in Greek flam-
ing fire, wailing, hatred and grief
Erebus: means darkness

Book XI (The Book of the Dead)

Following Circe's instructions, Odysseus summons up the spirits of the
dead. He speaks first to Tiresias who warns him to avoid harming the
oxen of the Sun, tells him of trouble at home, and prophesies his
future. He then speaks with his mother Anticleia who tells him about
his father Laertes and about Penelope. There follows the catalogue of
famous women. After this he pauses in his narration. Arete recom-
mends that he be given more gifts. Alcinous enquires whether he saw
any of his heroic comrades from the Trojan campaign. Odysseus then
tells of his meeting with Agamemnon, Achilles and Ajax, and his sight-
ing of other famous heroes.

NOTES AND GLOSSARY:
Cimmerians: possibly meaning dwellers in darkness
Elpenor: there is an apparent inconsistency here. Odysseus
asks him how he died, having already given the cir-
cumstances of his death in the previous book.
Elpenor asks to be cremated, the usual way of dis-
posing of the dead in Homer
Anticleia: Odysseus had been told by Circe not to speak to
anyone before Tiresias
Autolycus: a son of Hermes and Odysseus's grandfather,
renowned for his cunning and for thieving (see
XIX, 394–6)
Thrinacie: see XII, 260 for the beginning of this episode
Tiresias and the suitors: the prophecy is given three years after Odys-
seus left Troy, and the suitors did not begin to woo
Penelope until later. This anachronism has been
used in the argument against Homeric authorship
of XI
Odysseus's future: nowhere else elucidated in Homer. It implies
further travels

the winnowing fan: a long pole with a shovel-shaped end with which the corn was thrown up against the wind to clear it of chaff. It resembled an oar in appearance

death from Artemis's arrows: evidently a formula for expressing a peaceful death

Odysseus enquires about his estate: as king of Ithaca he was accorded special rights in terms of land and entertainment. He was not the sole Ithacan chieftain (see VIII, 46 where sceptered nobles, twelve in number, attend Alcinous in council)

Odysseus attempts to embrace Anticleia: when he is unable to do so, she explains the Homeric conception of the after-life

the catalogue of women: all figures of a previous generation famous in heroic legend

Tyro: she was illustrious in her descendants. Her son Neleus was the father of Nestor. Aeson was the father of Jason who led the Argonauts in quest of the Golden Fleece

Enipeus: a river in Thessaly in northern Greece

Iolcus: also in Thessaly, the town from which Jason sailed in his ship the Argo on his quest for the Golden Fleece

Asopus: a river flowing through Boeotia

Amphitryon's son: Heracles is meant here

Epicaste: called Iocasta by later writers. Homer does not mention the self-blinding of Oedipus

Orchomenus: in Boeotia

the seer: who attempted to win Pero was Melampus, the ancestor of Theoclymenus whose history is given at XV, 224

Iphicles: one of the Argonauts

Leda: she was visited by Zeus in the form of a swan. The product of this union was Helen. Leda was also the mother of Clytemnestra by Tyndareus

Polydeuces: more familiar in his Roman name of Pollux

Pelion and Ossa: mountains in Thessaly. To pile Pelion on Ossa became proverbial

the son of Leto: Apollo

Phaedra: the daughter of Minos, wife of Theseus of Athens and step-mother of Hippolytus with whom she fell in love

Procris: daughter of Erechtheus king of Athens, an unfaithful wife

Ariadne: she helped Theseus, whom she loved, to find his way in the Labyrinth (a maze) by means of a thread, thus saving him from the Minotaur, a monster with the head of a bull. She was subsequently deserted by Theseus

Dionysus: the god of wine, seldom mentioned in Homer

Maera: a nymph who devoted herself to Artemis, who killed her when she broke her vow of chastity

Eriphyle: when bribed with a gold necklace by Polyneices son of Oedipus, she persuaded her husband Amphiarous to join the expedition of the Seven Against Thebes on which he was doomed to die

Odysseus solicits gifts: gifts bring honour and esteem. He approves of Penelope's attempt to extract gifts from the suitors at XVIII, 281–3

Cassandra: allotted to Agamemnon as a spoil of war

Achilles on death: this is particularly poignant coming from him as he had been given a choice of a long life without distinction or a short one with achievement and fame. He chose the latter (*Iliad* IX, 410–16)

Phthia: the home town of Achilles in Thessaly. The fate of Peleus here reminds us of Laertes, in the same way that mention of Clytemnestra brought Penelope to mind

Scyros: according to later accounts Achilles's mother Thetis had disguised him as a girl and introduced him to the daughters of Lycomedes of Scyros (an island in the Aegean) under the name of Pyrrha so that he would not fight in the Trojan War. However, one of his companions bore Pyrrhus by him, thus uncovering his identity

asphodel: a lean spiky plant

the silence of Ajax: a famous moment, described as an example of sublimity in the treatise of the rhetorician Longinus (first century AD) *On the Sublime* IX, 2. Ajax had quarrelled with Odysseus over the arms of Achilles (see Book VIII)

Minos: king of Crete in life and a judge in the underworld

Orion: an active figure in contrast to those described previously. For this reason this passage is suspected to be a later interpolation. It has been thought strange that Odysseus can view scenes within the underworld. Prior to this the spirits have been coming to him

Tityos:	has the same punishment accorded in Greek myth to Prometheus (the god who brought mankind fire)
Tantalus:	according to some accounts he divulged the secrets of Zeus. In other accounts he abused the hospitality of the gods, hence his punishment. The word tantalise is derived from his fate
Sisyphus:	legend is not as clear about the original crime as it is about his subsequent punishment
Heracles:	he was immortalised by the gods
Hebe:	usually a cupbearer for the gods. Her name suggests the bloom of youth
Heracles's speech:	the master was Eurystheus for whom he was forced to carry out his twelve labours because of Hera's jealousy – he was a son of Zeus but not by her. One of his labours was the task of capturing Cerberus, a monstrous three-headed dog who guarded the gates of Hades
Pirithous and Theseus:	famous in legend for their friendship
Gorgon's head:	in later accounts the Gorgons had snakes writhing in their hair and faces which could turn men to stone

---

Book XII (The Sirens, Scylla and Charybdis. The Oxen of the Sun)

Circe, to whom he has returned, tells him of dangers to come. So that he can hear the song of the Sirens he instructs his men to bind him to the mast while sealing their own ears with wax. He sails between Scylla and Charybdis; Scylla seizes six of his men. They come to Thrinacie where they are marooned for a month by unfavourable winds. When food has run out his men, against his instructions, kill the oxen of the Sun when Odysseus is asleep. Zeus wrecks the fleet with a thunderbolt. Odysseus alone survives and drifts to the island of Ogygia.

NOTES AND GLOSSARY:

the Sirens:	two in number
the Argo:	the ship in which Jason sailed with the Argonauts (those who sailed in the Argo). Jason belonged to the previous generation of heroes
Aeetes:	Circe's brother who ruled in Colchis in the Black Sea
Charybdis:	the name suggests wide-swallower. The ancients thought that these two monsters were to be located in the straits of Messina between Italy and Sicily
Cratais:	the name suggests force

Thrinacie: a legendary island. This is Odysseus's second warning. Tiresias gave the first

Phaethusa and Lampetie: their names suggest brightness

Odysseus tells his crew of the prophecies: but does not tell them about Scylla and he is not as clear as he could have been about the danger on Thrinacie

the Sirens' song: irresistibly offers Odysseus knowledge

Odysseus arms himself: ignoring Circe's advice. Homer preserves his independence in spite of the inevitability imparted by the use of prophecy

Eurylochus: again the troublemaker. He had been critical of Odysseus before at X, 431–7

Book XIII (Odysseus's Voyage from the Phaeacians and Arrival in Ithaca)

The Phaeacians convey Odysseus to Ithaca by night and deposit him on the shore, asleep. In the morning he wakes up and does not recognise the place. Athene appears in the guise of a young shepherd, and Odysseus asks her where he is. She enlightens him. In response to her questions he tells his first Cretan tale to conceal his identity, saying he is on the run having killed a man. Athene is amused and reveals herself. They hide the treasure. Athene disguises Odysseus as an old beggar and sets him on the road to the hut of his loyal steward Eumaeus.

NOTES AND GLOSSARY:

Odysseus prays for Arete: his last words, as his first words, are addressed to Arete, she who is prayed to or for

Phorycs: a minor sea deity

Naiads: usually fresh water spirits. Dryads inhabit trees, Oreads mountains and Nereids the sea

the cave of the nymphs: a strange description that has attracted bizarre interpretation. The cave was thought to be an allegory of the world by Porphyrius of Tyre, a writer of the third century AD

Odysseus left asleep on the shore: Homer has been much criticised for what has been regarded as an absurdity here

Poseidon's anger: he feels that he has been dishonoured. Zeus placates him. Both gods are somewhat malevolent here

Odysseus's concern for his treasure: the Homeric heroes have due regard for the material things of this world, whether it be feasting and drinking, of which there is much in the *Odyssey*, or amassing treasure of which there are also many tales

Athene describes Ithaca: compare the description of Telemachus at IV, 600–8

the Cretan tale: the first of several told by Odysseus. The Cretans besides being great traders and adventurers were also proverbial liars

Orsilochus: means ambush-causer

Sidon: in Phoenicia, now the Lebanon

Athene reluctant to oppose Poseidon: Homer explains here why the goddess does not appear in the narrative of his wanderings

Arethusa: a Nereid, a sea nymph. Nereus was a god of the sea

Book XIV (The Conversation of Odysseus with Eumaeus)

Eumaeus welcomes the stranger at his door, feeds him, complains about the suitors, and asks Odysseus about himself. His master in reply tells his second Cretan tale, saying he had heard of Odysseus in Thesprotia. Eumaeus does not believe this, but continues to treat him well. Odysseus tells a second tale of a night ambush at Troy in order to elicit a cloak and tunic from Eumaeus.

NOTES AND GLOSSARY:

Eumaeus welcomes Odysseus: it is not *themis*, he says, to dishonour strangers, for all strangers and beggars are under the protection of Zeus (compare with the Cyclopes' attitude to *themis* in IX). Homer quickly establishes the character of Eumaeus and a key moral issue in the second half of the poem

Eumaeus condemns the suitors: their wooing of Penelope violates *dike*, right and customary conduct

Odysseus's wealth: he owns land on the mainland too

Arceisius: Odysseus's paternal grandfather, a son of Zeus

the second Cretan tale: Odysseus represents himself as an adventurer, entrepreneur and money-maker (compare Menelaus in IV)

Thesprotia: to the north of Ithaca on the Greek mainland

Pheidon: the name means he who spares

Dodona: in Epirus, the site of the oldest and most famous oracle of Zeus always associated with the oak trees that grew there

death by sea: compare the lament of Telemachus (I, 234–40) and of Odysseus himself (V, 299–312)

Aetolia: a district in the south-west of the Greek mainland north of the Peloponnese

Maia:	a daughter of Atlas who gave birth to Hermes, a child of Zeus, on Mount Cyllene in Arcadia. Hermes was the god of herdsmen
Mesaulius:	the name means yardman. Eumaeus has his own servants so that he is a figure of authority in the household of Odysseus
Taphians:	a neighbouring people who traded by sea. Athene disguises herself as a Taphian sailor in Book I, and Penelope reminds Antinous that Odysseus had saved his father from Taphian pirates (XVI, 424–30)

Eumaeus gives Odysseus night clothing: but he is no fool, and has seen through Odysseus's motives in telling the tale

---

Book XV (The Arrival of Telemachus at Eumaeus's Hut)

Telemachus makes preparations to return to Ithaca from his expedition to Pylos and Sparta. He gives passage to Theoclymenus, who is a man on the run as a result of a homicide. Eumaeus tells Odysseus about his father Laertes and relates his own history. Telemachus returns.

NOTES AND GLOSSARY:

Menelaus's speech to Telemachus:	famous for its typically Greek emphasis on moderation in all things (nothing in excess) and also for its proverbial line about the welcoming of the coming guest and the speeding of the departing guest
Megapenthes:	the name means great grief. He is the son of Menelaus by a slave girl. Helen could not bear him a son. By her he has a daughter Hermione (see IV, 110–14)

an eagle on the right: the right side is auspicious in Greek folklore

Pherae:	halfway between Sparta and Pylos. They return by the way they came

the history of Melampus: see also XI, 281–97. The relevance and point of this long history have often been questioned

a woman's avarice: Eriphyle mentioned at XI, 326

Theoclymenus:	the name means god-famed. It seems to be the regular Homeric practice that retribution for a homicide was a matter for the immediate kinsmen of the slain. In the *Iliad* Ajax remarks that gifts can expiate a homicide so that compensation might settle the issue on occasion (IX, 632–7)

Chalcis: a river south of the Alpheus in Elis. The place
                  names mentioned here have been located on the
                  coast south of Ithaca
Ctimene: Odysseus's sister, only mentioned here. Her hus-
                  band gave gifts for her as Eurymachus hopes to do
                  for Penelope (XV, 17–18)
Same: a neighbouring island
sorrows recalled with pleasure: a famous sentiment
Syrie: identified with Delos
Eurymachus the best of the suitors: not necessarily in character, but in
                  wealth and fortune

Book XVI (The Recognition of Odysseus by Telemachus)

Telemachus arrives at Eumaeus's hut where he meets the stranger
whom he tells of the situation in the palace. He asks Eumaeus to go to
the palace to tell Penelope that he has returned safely. Odysseus then
reveals himself to his son. Together they plot the destruction of the
suitors. When the suitors hear that Telemachus has eluded their
ambush, they discuss Antinous's suggestion that he be waylaid before
he reaches the palace. Penelope, informed by Medon, hears of this dis-
cussion and roundly rebukes them. Eurymachus makes a soothing
speech. Eumaeus returns to his hut and reports to Telemachus.

NOTES AND GLOSSARY:
like a father welcoming his son: a highly apposite simile
Medon: the name means protector. One of the few noble-
                  men loyal to Odysseus, he informs Penelope of the
                  plot against her son
Telemachus modifies the plan: he is shrewd. Too much testing might
                  delay matters or alert the suitors
Antinous fears public opinion: for the first time the suitors are on the
                  defensive, having been outwitted by Telemachus
Amphinomous: the most intelligent and sympathetic of the suitors.
                  His advice shows political shrewdness.

Book XVII (The Return of Telemachus to the Palace)

Telemachus goes to the palace and is welcomed by Eumaeus and Pene-
lope. The prophet Theoclymenus declares that Odysseus has already
returned home. Telemachus tells Penelope of his journey. Odysseus
sets out for the palace and is insulted by the goatherd Melantheus.
Odysseus is recognised by his old dog Argus. He enters the palace and
proceeds to beg from the suitors. Antinous in anger throws a stool at

him. Eumaeus tells Penelope that the stranger claims to have seen Odysseus. Penelope asks to see him.

NOTES AND GLOSSARY:

Telemachus rebukes Penelope: for the second time (compare I, 346–61). Again Penelope is taken aback

Mentor: a wise counsellor and supporter of Telemachus

Halitherses: the soothsayer who had prophesied the doom of the suitors in the first Ithacan assembly

Telemachus and his treasure: like his father, he makes careful provision for his goods

Penelope to Telemachus: throughout the poem there is some tension between son and mother

Medon: he has a foot in both camps

Ithacus: it is to be presumed that he gave his name to Ithaca, just as Neritus gave his name to the mountain

Melantheus: the one man servant of Odysseus who proved disloyal; a foil to Eumaeus

Argus: the name means swift. The ship Argo is appropriately named. Argus's neglect has symbolic force, though the details are fully natural

Antinous to Eumaeus: a fine sarcasm in his speech here

Telemachus to Antinous: he returns the sarcasm

the stranger to Antinous: Odysseus tells him a shortened version of the Cretan tale he told to Eumaeus with a slight variation at the end

Dmetor: the name means he who subdues

Penelope's cry: this introduces the motif of the bow

Telemachus's sneeze: an omen

Book XVIII (The Boxing Match of Odysseus and Irus)

The suitors entertain themselves by provoking a sparring match between the stranger and the beggar Irus. Odysseus warns Amphinomus of the retribution awaiting the suitors. Penelope appears before the suitors to elicit gifts from them. Odysseus is insulted by a maidservant Melantho, and mocked by Eurymachus who throws a stool at him. Telemachus intervenes to bring peace to the palace.

NOTES AND GLOSSARY:

Irus: the winged messenger of the gods is called Iris. A pun is intended in this nickname (see also line 73). His real name is Arnaeus

the urges of the belly: Odysseus makes much of this (compare VII, 216–7; XVII, 286–9; 473–4)

Echetus: a figure from folk tale
Odysseus warns Amphinomus: who is the most intelligent and best intentioned of the suitors
Telemachus's beard: crucial to the plot (see Odysseus's instructions to Penelope before he left for Troy, line 269)
Penelope rebukes Telemachus: they are typically at odds with one another. Telemachus's reply shows the hastiness of Penelope's speech
Penelope solicits gifts: her action appeals to Odysseus's acquisitive sense
Melantho: sister of Melantheus and equally villainous
Eurymachus throws a stool: as Antinous had at XVII, 462. On this occasion, however, the taunting comes first from the suitor
Amphinomus makes the peace: he is again the politic suitor

Book XIX (The Conversation of Odysseus and Penelope. The Recognition by Eurycleia)

Odysseus and Telemachus remove the arms from the hall. Odysseus is insulted by Melantho again and roundly rebukes her. He talks to Penelope who tells him how she put off the suitors with the device of the web. Odysseus tells her his Cretan tale and predicts that her husband will soon return. He is washed by Eurycleia who recognises him from the scar that he acquired in his boyhood. She is sworn to secrecy. Penelope tells the stranger of a dream which he interprets favourably. She then announces her decision to stage the contest with the bow.

NOTES AND GLOSSARY:
instructions about arms: repeated from XVI, 281–98
the light in the hall: omens and divine signs are used by Homer with increasing frequency as the climax approaches
Odysseus rebukes Melantho: one of the great moral themes of the poem partly repeated from XVII, 419–24
the web: first mentioned by Antinous at II, 94–107
the third Cretan tale: almost the same (in shortened form) as the fiction narrated to Eumaeus at XIV, 199–359 and Antinous at XVII, 415–44
Crete a rich land: Crete was the centre of a developed civilisation called Minoan from the mythical king Minos, mentioned below
the peoples of Crete: they are all historical
Cnossus: the capital of Crete and the site of famous archaeological discoveries in the late nineteenth century

Malea: the most easterly promontory of the Peloponnese where Odysseus had been blown off course in his wanderings (IX, 80)

Amnisus: the port of Cnossus

Eileithyie: the goddess of childbirth

Odysseus's clothes: a striking picture suggesting opulence and power in marked contrast to his present condition

the brooch: richly described and typical of the sophisticated art works represented in the Homeric poems, the most notable of which is the shield of Achilles in the *Iliad*. Note also the work basket of Helen (IV, 128–32) and the doors of the palace of Alcinous (VII, 88–94). All such descriptions contribute to the impression of material beauty and splendour characteristic of the heroic age

Eurybates the squire: the description of him throws the beauty of Odysseus into relief

travel in pursuit of wealth: once again a picture of Odysseus the acquisitive (compare Menelaus's seven year travels at III, 301-2). He tactfully avoids mention of Calypso

a bath for the stranger: creature comforts are prized throughout the *Odyssey*. There is nothing Spartan (in the later sense of ascetic) about Homeric man. Here, of course, the washing advances the plot

Penelope on fame: only a good reputation can survive death; hence the impulse to excel, characteristic of the Homeric hero

the scar: a celebrated episode

Odysseus's name: *odussomai* means I hate

Parnassus: a mountain above Delphi in central Greece

Pandareus: a king of Crete. His daughter Aedon married Zethus king of Thebes. She had only one son Itylus. Jealous of the many children of Niobe, her sister-in-law, she planned to kill the eldest, but killed her own son by mistake. Zeus in pity changed her into a nightingale so that as such she melodiously laments the death of Itylus

Penelope's dilemma: Telemachus's coming of age is the new factor pressing upon her

Penelope's dream: is cunningly conceived by Homer. In the dream she mourns the loss of her geese, whereas for the audience it is an omen of her good fortune to come. A fine example of the irony that pervades the second half of the poem

the contest with the bow: the arrow is to go through twelve axes. Commentators have much debated the precise meaning of this without coming to a convincing conclusion.

Book XX (Events before the Suitor-slaying)

Odysseus witnesses the immorality of some of his maidservants as they depart to sleep with the suitors. Odysseus is awakened by the sounds of Penelope's distress and prays for a favourable omen. Zeus thunders in a cloudless sky. Preparations begin for the festival of Apollo. Odysseus is insulted by Ctesippus who throws a cow's hoof at him. A supernatural scene at the banquet of the suitors is interpreted by Theoclymenus to be prophetic of their doom. They carry on feasting obliviously.

NOTES AND GLOSSARY:

Odysseus like a black pudding: a notorious simile
death from Artemis: Penelope prays for a quick release from her suffering
daughters of Pandareus: apparently punished for their father's sin of stealing an artefact made by Hephaestus from the temple of Zeus in Crete
Eurycleia as housekeeper: she is in charge of the other female servants. Like Eumaeus she is of noble birth
Philoetius: he is to help in the final encounter. In this book the effect of Odysseus's absence upon his servants is felt
Cephallenia: a neighbouring island, or possibly a general name for the surrounding area (see XXIV, 355; 378)
a bird on the left: a sinister omen
Amphinomus: the most intelligent of the suitors
sacred feast: it is appropriate that the archery contest should take place on a day sacred to the archer god
Ctesippus throws a cow's hoof: this is the third such incident (compare XVII, 462 and XVIII, 394). This time the action is entirely unprovoked
Telemachus no longer a child: again a matter for emphasis
Theoclymenus's vision: compare the light in the hall at XIX, 33–40. But this is the only prophetic vision in the Homeric poems

Book XXI (The Contest with the Bow)

Penelope descends to a storeroom to find the bow, and promises to marry the man who can string it and successfully shoot an arrow

through a row of twelve axes. The axes are set up. One of the suitors
tries and fails. Odysseus reveals himself to Eumaeus and to Philoetius a
loyal herdsman. When Eurymachus fails to string the bow, Antinous
suggests that they postpone the contest until the following day. Odys-
seus asks if he can try his hand. Eumaeus brings him the bow which he
successfully strings, and then shoots an arrow through the twelve axes.
Telemachus arms himself and stands by his father.

NOTES AND GLOSSARY:

Penelope's hand: is described in the Homeric formula as *pacheie*,
thick or sturdy, an epithet which is usually thought
to be inappropriate for a woman of grace and
beauty

Iphitus: another tale involving piracy and homicide

Eurytus: a famous bowman, reputedly the teacher of
Heracles

Odysseus reveals himself: to Philoetius and Eumaeus, having once
again tested them just at the opportune time

Eurytion the Centaur: the Centaurs were human to the waist and horse
below it. The drunk Eurytion tried to carry off the
bride at the marriage of Pirithous and Hippoda-
mia, thus starting the battle of the Lapiths and the
Centaurs

Telemachus dismisses Penelope: for the third time (see also I, 346−61
and XVII, 44−56). This is the strongest of his
assertions at the climactic moment

a ship's cable made of *biblos*: that is from the Egyptian papyrus from
which books *biblia* (whence Bible) were later made

Book XXII (The Suitor-slaying)

Odysseus kills Antinous and reveals himself to the suitors. Eury-
machus offers to make amends and begs for mercy; Odysseus kills him.
Amphinomus falls to the spear of Telemachus. Father and son set
about the rest of the suitors. Through Melantheus the suitors acquire
some arms and put up some resistance. All but Phemius and Medon are
killed. Eurycleia is sent for. The twelve erring maidservants are ordered
to clear up the hall and then they are hanged. Melantheus is killed and
mutilated. The hall is purified. Eurycleia is sent to tell Penelope of
these events.

NOTES AND GLOSSARY:

Eurymachus confesses: the suitors' guilt is never at issue in the poem

twenty oxen: a large sum, which Laertes had paid for Eurycleia
(I, 431)

Athene in the guise of Mentor: Odysseus had entrusted his house to his friend Mentor on his departure (see II, 224−8). He rebukes the people of Ithaca in the assembly for not opposing the suitors. Athene takes his form again at the end of the poem (XXIV, 502)

the death of Ctesippus: his death at the hands of the cowman is a grim piece of poetic justice since he had thrown a cow's hoof at Odysseus (XX, 299)

the aegis: literally a storm cloud, it is a heavy shield with a hundred gold tassels, the means of creating panic among mortals

Phemius: called here Terpiades, the son of delight; the priest's plea for mercy goes unheeded, but Odysseus spares the bard who promises to lay his art at his master's disposal

Medon: he is lucky to escape because, although he tells Penelope of the plot against Telemachus, he also joined in the revelry (see XVI, 412 and XVII, 172−3)

Eurycleia's cry: incurs a famous rebuke. The heroes of the *Iliad* always exult over the slain. Perhaps there is the feeling here that the suitors are not worth boasting over, or that as their death is a just punishment the sense of triumph that is proper over a defeat of an equal is improper here

the hanging of the maids: a dishonorable death for dishonorable conduct

the death of Melantheus: the barbarities are not perpetrated by Odysseus.

Book XXIII (The Recognition of Odysseus by Penelope)

Eurycleia tells Penelope what has happened. Penelope expresses disbelief which is not dispelled when she confronts Odysseus. He is patient with her and makes plans to avoid news of the killing from reaching the outside world. After testing her husband, Penelope becomes convinced of the truth. Odysseus tells her of his wanderings, after which they spend the night together. Next morning he prepares to set off to his father's farm.

NOTES AND GLOSSARY:

Telemachus rebukes Penelope: son and mother are at odds again. The temper and experience of father and son are contrasted in this scene

Odysseus on homicide: the Aetolian stranger (XIV, 380) and Theo-
clymenus (XV, 224) have fled their country after a
homicide. Compare also the fictitious Cretan tale
at XIII, 259. Retribution for a homicide is a matter
for the kinsmen of the slain; there is no external
authority. It is characteristic of Odysseus to weigh
consequences

Athene beautifies Odysseus: repeated from VI, 230–5

the secret of the bed: a skilful test of Odysseus by Penelope. She is
the only mortal to get the better of him and to pro-
voke him to an unconsidered outburst

Actoris: not mentioned elsewhere

the simile of the safe landing: most apt; Penelope as much as Odysseus
has been through the seas of adversity

Lampus and Phaethon: both names suggest shining light. The Dawn is
drawn across the sky in a horse-drawn chariot

Odysseus's final journey: partly to appease the wrath of Poseidon

Odysseus tells of his wanderings: he offers a summary of his story in
chronological sequence

restoration of Odysseus's resources: by plundering, evidently the cus-
tomary practice in Homeric society.

Book XXIV (Truce)

Hermes escorts the souls of the suitors to Hades. The spirit of
Agamemnon is surprised to see such a number and asks Amphimedon
to give an account of their death. On hearing his story, Agamemnon
praises the action of Odysseus and extols the virtue of Penelope. Odys-
seus visits Laertes to whom he tells a false story before finally revealing
his identity to their mutual rejoicing. The Ithacans in council, after
hearing of the deaths of the suitors, decide to do battle with Odysseus.
Laertes, Odysseus and Telemachus begin the fight which is stopped by
Athene, who commands the peace.

NOTES AND GLOSSARY:

Cyllenian: Hermes was born on Mount Cyllene in Arcadia

his wand: compare V, 47–8. In later literature he is called
psychopompos, the escort of souls (from *pompe*
procession and *psyche* spirit or soul)

the White Rock: this has occasioned much inconclusive debate; it is
not referred to in other descriptions of the
approach to Hades

the gates of the sun: in the extreme west where the sun sets

Agamemnon and Achilles: they are reconciled here. In the *Iliad* they
are at odds

Achilles's mother: the sea-goddess Thetis
Hellespont: the narrow strait between the Trojan plain and the Thracian Chersonese now dividing Europe from Asia
funeral games for Achilles: there are funeral games for Patroclus in *Iliad* XXIII
the web of Penelope: this is the third account. Antinous complains about Penelope's conduct in the Ithacan assembly (II, 94–107) and Penelope tells the stranger (XIX, 137–56)
Amphimedon tells of the suitor-slaying: he believes that Odysseus instigated the contest with the bow
Agamemnon praises Penelope: a dramatic culmination to this underworld interview
king of the Cephallenians: this implies all the subjects ruled by Odysseus in Ithaca and elsewhere on neighbouring islands and the mainland
Nerikos: in Leucas
Dolius: the father of Melantheus and Melantho
Eupeithes: the name means plausible
Zeus calls for a happy ending: for friendship, wealth and peace

Part 3

Commentary

Structure and plot

The beginning

The opening lines provide a summary of the story of Odysseus, the storm-tossed and resourceful wanderer famous in legend for his 'Odyssey', his journey to strange lands and distant places undertaken after the sack of Troy. Before he reached Ithaca he underwent many hardships in the course of which his comrades perished through their own folly, having eaten the oxen of Hyperion the Sun (I, 1–10). It is to be presumed that these lines summarise what Odysseus was already famous for in Homer's day, and their function is simply to bring that famous story to mind, for Homer bids his muse begin the tale of Odysseus at any point she wishes. In the event, Homer's muse does not make the subject of the prologue the centre of the main action of the poem. The loss of Odysseus's comrades, far from being central, is a mere episode narrated in little more than one hundred lines (XII, 265–375). Homer starts the *Odyssey* at a point when Odysseus's 'Odyssey' is almost over, long after he has lost his comrades, when he has been the prisoner of the nymph Calypso on the island of Ogygia for seven years. Hermes is despatched to free Odysseus; he makes a twenty day journey to Scherie where he is entertained by the Phaeacians for three days and escorted back overnight to Ithaca, his journey's end coming halfway through the poem (XIII, 113). Paradoxically the 'Odyssey' of Odysseus, if the term is taken to mean a great journey, is not the centre of Homer's *Odyssey* at all. The main part of the wanderings of Odysseus come in the form of an interlude in the retrospective narrative given by Odysseus to the Phaeacians in his after-dinner speech (Books IX–XII). The remainder of the poem, its second half, is entirely concerned with the situation in Ithaca with which the poem opened and with Odysseus's successful efforts to regain the mastery of his own household. In the *Odyssey*, therefore, Homer's principal subject is the final homecoming of Odysseus and the steps he must take to restore order in Ithaca.

To this end, Homer distinguishes Odysseus from the rest of the Greek heroes who have already returned home by the time the poem opens. Odysseus, alone and still longing for his return and his wife, is imprisoned by the nymph Calypso on the island of Ogygia (I, 11–15).

Athene further tells us that Odysseus, in resisting the blandishments of the nymph and yearning for the sight of the smoke rising from Ithaca, longs to die (I, 48−59). When Hermes visits Calypso, Odysseus is weeping on the shore as he gazes out to sea (V, 82−4). Having chosen to begin at the end of Odysseus's long journey, Homer concentrates upon one single emotion, upon nostalgia in its literal meaning, upon the desire of Odysseus and of his loyal household for the hero's homecoming; for the nostalgia of Odysseus has its counterpart in the 'long hope' of his family (XXIII, 54) that Odysseus will one day return.

The poem starts with a dramatic representation of the disorder in Ithaca in the absence of Odysseus. The precise state of affairs has puzzled cultural historians who have tried to disentangle a credible social reality from the poetic fiction. Although it has long been fashionable to stress the commemorative function of the Homeric bard in transmitting knowledge of the social customs and manners of time past, Homer is primarily a poet with a story to tell or rather a plot to organise, so that precision of the kind likely to appeal to the social historian is not to be expected. Furthermore he unfolds his tale through direct speech and action giving only such information as is dramatically appropriate. When Athene in disguise as a stranger asks Telemachus what is happening in his house (I, 222−8) he gives a brief outline likely to satisfy the curious outsider. Odysseus his father has vanished from the face of the earth without a trace and is presumed dead. All the sons of the neighbouring aristocracy are competing for the hand of his mother Penelope in marriage and eating him out of house and home. The facts of the situation, necessary for the plot, are clear. The choice lies with Penelope, and the wooers will press their suit until she chooses one of their number. In the Ithacan assembly the youthful Telemachus rebukes the suitors for not having the courage to go directly to Penelope's father so that he could make terms with the man of his choice (II, 50−4). The suitors reply that it is up to Telemachus to send his mother back to her father's house himself (II, 113−14; 195−7). This Telemachus for reasons both financial and moral is unwilling to do. Here is an impasse, but the situation is not static. Telemachus has called an assembly in an attempt to raise support for the ejection of the suitors, but the suitors are in no mood to go, and the people of Ithaca are entirely passive. Nor is there in Homeric society any external authority to which appeal can be made. In the circumstances there is little that the young Telemachus can do. The suitors have been besieging Penelope for a number of years and he, an only son, has only recently come to manhood. When Penelope rebukes Phemius for singing of the return of the Greeks from Troy, a song which causes her pain, she is greatly surprised when Telemachus rebukes her in turn and bids her retire to her room (I, 346−61). Telemachus is beginning to assert himself, but he lacks authority,

experience and adequate support. His tears in the assembly are tears of
frustration that in his inexperience he is unable to control (II, 80−1).
Nevertheless his undertaking to seek word of his father to bring the un-
certainty to an end is a decisive act designed to bring matters to a head,
and it is the means by which Homer sets his plot in motion.

The position of Penelope is similarly delicate. Her stratagem with
the web which has delayed matters for nearly four years has been dis-
covered. Wishing to remain loyal to Odysseus, she does not want to
choose a successor, but the assertion of Telemachus which exposes him
to danger puts new pressure upon her. The danger to Telemachus is not
an idle fancy. The suitors, sensing that he will cause difficulty, plot his
death by ambush on his return from Sparta. He is only able to elude
them by use of his wits. The situation in Ithaca at the opening of the
poem is, therefore, most unstable; events are taking an ugly turn and
entering a dangerous and critical phase.

The journey to Pylos and Sparta widens the scope of the poem
beyond the confines of Ithaca by taking us back in time to the Trojan
War, by recounting the fate of other heroes on their return and by pro-
viding a contrasting picture of other Greek households. Telemachus
seeks knowledge of Odysseus's whereabouts (given to him by Menelaus
in Book IV) but Homer, through the reminiscences of old comrades,
tells us of the strategic role of Odysseus in the heroic enterprise at Troy,
and chiefly of the parallel sufferings undergone by the rest of the
Greeks returning from Troy. The fate of Agamemnon, killed in
ambush by the usurper Aegisthus, exposes the dangerous position of
the war heroes returning to the different insecurities of a post-war
world. The retrospective narratives are largely concerned with the suf-
ferings of the past, but in present time the stable worlds of Pylos and
Sparta represent the orderly values and customary manners of peace-
time civilisation that are so conspicuously flouted in the chaotic and
disorderly state of Ithaca. The simple piety of Nestor and the old hero's
relationship with his sons, the humanity of Menelaus and his tranquil
relationship with Helen, and above all the hospitality, entertainment
and gifts bestowed upon Telemachus are all evidence of Homeric civili-
sation at its best. Both Nestor and Menelaus express abhorrence at
what is happening in Ithaca. The ignoble plot against Telemachus at
the end of Book IV is in sudden and marked contrast to the elevated
moral tone of proceedings at Pylos and Sparta.

Whatever rights the suitors have in the case, the judgement upon
them is clear. It is apparent in the reaction of Athene right at the outset
(I, 253−66) and confirmed later in the outrage of Nestor and Menelaus.
The insolence of the suitors and their lack of restraint are repeatedly
stressed. Their riotous actions and insulting speeches are a gross breach
of Homeric manners. The line between unseemly behaviour and down-

right wickedness is clearly crossed in the plot to ambush and kill Telemachus. In the sarcastic taunting that greets Telemachus's request for a ship, Homer gives us a glimpse into the workings of the suitors' minds. One of their number remarks that perhaps Telemachus will be lost on his journey like his father. Then they will be left with the onerous task of dividing his property between them and presenting his house to his mother and her new husband (II, 332−6). With Telemachus out of the way, there will be something for everybody not just for the lucky man chosen by Penelope. The iniquity of the suitors is further suggested in the angry outburst of Leiocritus to the effect that even if Odysseus were to return, he would meet with a sticky end (II, 242−51).

The suitors are a bad lot and are to meet their just deserts. Predicting their doom Athene specifically says that they are witless and unjust (II, 282). The issue of justice is obliquely apparent in the opening speech of Zeus in which he condemns Aegisthus for his folly in murdering Agamemnon. Athene holds up Orestes, who avenged his father, as a model to Telemachus who must be equally brave (I, 296−302). Nestor and Menelaus take a similarly uncomplicated view of the rights and wrongs of Agamemnon's case (in marked contrast to the later dramatist Aeschylus (525/4−456BC) in *The Oresteian Trilogy*). The omen sent by Zeus during the Ithacan council is interpreted by the soothsayer as a clear warning to the suitors which they rudely ignore rather in the way that Aegisthus had ignored the warning of Hermes (I, 32−43). The suitors are to perish, as did the companions of Odysseus, by their own witlessness and folly. The contrasting idea we are given of Odysseus by his loyal household is one that associates him with all manner of virtue. Mentor tells us that he ruled his people like a loving father (II, 233−4). Penelope similarly calls him to mind as a just and benevolent ruler (IV, 687−93). The moral outline of the *Odyssey* is simple and clear. In the opening book, the stage is set for the ultimate triumph of good over evil in the poetic justice that is to be meted out in the reversal of fortune at the poem's climax.

In the opening books Homer has laid the groundwork for the development of his plot by introducing the characters who are the leading figures of the main action in such a way as to show how their fate and wellbeing are entirely dependent upon the return of Odysseus. Although the hero is not present in the opening, there is a great expectation of him; he is constantly in view and in the fraught situation in Ithaca we see how all depends upon his absence and upon the uncertainty surrounding his return. The sufferings of his family and household are a counterpart of the sufferings of Odysseus himself; in fact the sufferings of family and hero are two facets of a single set of circumstances united in a simple chain of cause and effect. Such is the simple unity underlying the action at the beginning of the poem. Yet Homer complicates and diversifies his plot by starting with the self-assertion and journey of Telemachus. He has, as it were, a double string to his bow. The self-assertion and journey are too much a part of the main design and too well integrated into the main action to constitute what could accurately be called a double or sub-plot. Homer's art achieves a more subtle unity. There is something very artful, too, in beginning a poem about a homecoming with a journey outwards away from home. To use a musical metaphor, this is a contrapuntal move. In counterpoint, which is more artful and surprising than simple melody, two tunes are combined so that they can be played together as a single theme. In interweaving the double strands of his plot Homer achieves a comparable effect.

Homecoming and retrospect

Telemachus leaves home to find news of his father. Menelaus tells him of the prophecy of Proteus that Odysseus is imprisoned on Calypso's island. There is a natural and easy transition to our first encounter with Odysseus on Ogygia in Book V. We join him at the nadir of his fortunes, alone and tearful. Given the point in his story at which he begins, Homer can draw a discreet veil over what is not to his purpose, Odysseus's relationship with Calypso with whom he has been living for seven years. He shows the love of the goddess for the hero, but it is all one-sided. Odysseus is apart from the goddess, yearning for his return home. All the focus is upon that return, upon the preparations necessary for it and on the hardships undergone in the first stage of it during the storm on the way to Scherie. Odysseus's emergence from the storm to the tranquil land of the Phaeacians is a further masterly transition on the part of Homer. The meeting with Nausicaa contrasts with the relationship with the goddess and is a charming and delightful episode in itself, but it also contributes to the main design. Odysseus, a stranger in a foreign land, needs to win the confidence of the Phaeacians if he is to complete his journey home. Nausicaa effects his welcome to the palace where he is entertained by the king and queen.

Scherie is an idealised and romantic island, well suited to the chief function it is to serve as the setting for Odysseus's account of his fabulous adventures. Homer describes the Phaeacians as kinsmen of the gods (V, 35). Scherie is cut off from the haunts of men (VI, 8). It is a kind of natural paradise, a rich land whose inhabitants know of war only as a subject of song while pursuing the occupations of peace. The striking descriptions of the magnificent palace and of the beautiful garden (VII, 84–132) evoke a world of order, harmony and proportion, a cultivated place of material splendour in which the physical and the artistic are valued and celebrated. Odysseus joins in the games and is treated to the pleasures of song and dance. The blind bard Demodocus holds an honoured place among the Phaeacians. There is an air of general benevolence throughout; in the delicate manners exhibited in the royal household between king, queen and princess, and in the generous hospitality shown to Odysseus who arrives as a stranger in their midst. The good sense, amiability and piety of the Phaeacians recall Pylos and Sparta, but Scherie is a more tranquil world, not imbued like Pylos and Sparta with an aura of past suffering and regret. Into this tranquil world the suffering spirit of Odysseus is almost an intrusion, providing a piquant contrast between felicity and calamity comparable to the contrast between youth and experience that characterises the encounters of Telemachus with Nestor and Menelaus. With a fine irony Odysseus is entertained with the song of his own quarrel with Achilles at Troy. Homer keeps his identity secret until the end of Book VIII where it is discovered by another stroke of art when Alcinous notices his tearful reaction to a second Trojan story sung by Demodocus, the stratagem of the Wooden Horse devised by Odysseus himself. In answer to the king's enquiry he gives the account of his wanderings from Troy in the form of an after-dinner entertainment.

The retrospective narrative of the hero's past wanderings enables Homer to give concentration to the present action of his poem. It also makes it possible for him to incorporate folk tales and folk motifs into his poem in such a way as to minimise any clash between the two orders of reality represented by Ithaca and the folk world. There are folk motifs incorporated into the Ithacan narratives such as the web of Penelope and even the device of the great bow itself, but the first of these is already in the past by the time of the present action, and the second is narrated with all possible realism. The tales involving the Lotus-eaters, the Cyclops, Circe, the Sirens, and Scylla and Charybdis have more magic, mystery and romance than would have been compatible with the realistic present action of Ithaca. Having decided to make such extensive use of old folk tales (Homer could have made Odysseus's wanderings as realistic as the Cretan tales in the second half of the poem) it was a fine stroke of judgement to isolate and enclose them altogether in an after-dinner speech. When he begins his narrative, Odysseus remarks that there is nothing sweeter than when the banqueters listen to the bard at a full feast when the wine flows freely (IX, 2–11). The wanderings are therefore given a special status as tales of entertainment after the reality of present daytime activity. This has a subtle effect. Homer takes similar care to isolate the fabulous tales that Menelaus tells Telemachus at Sparta in an after-dinner speech. As if to prepare us for the change to a different order of reality, Helen mixes a powerful anodyne with the wine that circulates before the tale (IV, 219–32). Having decided to isolate the fabulous wanderings in a retrospective narrative Homer could have made Eumaeus, Telemachus or Penelope the audience for such an entertainment. Instead he chose to have Odysseus give the recital in a world that is not unconnected with the fabulous world of the folk tales. The Phaeacians have magic ships and a special destiny decreed by the gods. Scherie is in fact Odysseus's last port of call in the world of romance before he returns to the down-to-earth realities of Ithaca. At the same time Scherie is nearer in a figurative as well as a literal sense to Ithaca than any other place visited by Odysseus in his wanderings. It is a fully human world in which the ideals of Greek culture are celebrated. It therefore functions as a bridge between the two orders of reality.

The account that Odysseus gives of his wanderings from Troy in four books, from IX to XII, might seem something of a digression from the main subject of the poem concerning his homecoming and re-establishment, but it is a necessary part of the whole since Odysseus must account for his long absence, and without such an account the poem would be incomplete. Even in earlier tales, like the episode of the Lotus-eaters which threatens to extinguish the desire to return home, and the encounter with the Cyclops which accounts for the hostility of Poseidon to Odysseus, there are links with the main subject. As the narrative progresses Homer gradually links the various episodes to the homecoming by the use of prophecy. Circe tells Odysseus that he must seek the spirit of the prophet Tiresias in the underworld. Tiresias warns him of the dangers ahead; in particular that he must take care not to harm the cattle of the Sun god. He prophesies trouble at home with the suitors of Penelope and further journeys for Odysseus. Then the spirit of Odysseus's mother Anticleia tells him about Penelope and her continued faithfulness. Odysseus makes the contrast with Helen, and the spirit of Agamemnon denounces the faithlessness of his wife Clytemnestra (XI, 421–34). The presence of the other Greek heroes who have been denied a successful return from Troy offers a poignant contrast to the saga of the living hero who is destined to return. In such ways the retrospective narrative is thematically linked to the main action. Finally Odysseus must explain how he came to lose his companions, and Homer arranges their demise in such a way as to exonerate his hero from all blame. They die despite his forewarnings and as a result of their own witlessness and folly. Their fate is a further manifestation of the poetic justice that runs throughout the *Odyssey*.

Whatever their function in relation to the past, the tales are also told as present entertainments and serve to enhance the character and status of the hero in his audience's estimation before he embarks upon his final encounter. When he pauses in the account of his underworld conversations, the Phaeacians are spellbound, and Arete praises the combination of physical and mental prowess in her guest exhorting her people to honour him with generous gifts (XI, 336–41). This they later do when Odysseus is sent back with a quantity of cauldrons, tripods, gold and fabric. Alcinous remarks that Odysseus has told his story with the skill of a minstrel (XI, 367–8). He had arrived at the palace a ship-wrecked and destitute stranger forced to beg his passage home. The welcome he receives springs from the natural benevolence of the Phaeacians, but through his feats in the games, and, above all, through his masterly recital, he earns more than the welcome due to strangers. He earns the honour due to him as the long-suffering man of many turns of fortune and sole survivor of a series of miraculous adventures. He returns to Ithaca at a point in the poem when his heroic status has been fully established and is accorded due recognition. The marvellous adventures are, therefore, artfully integrated in the poem by Homer in such a way as to enhance his hero in the present action, and give maximum impact to his return to Ithaca. A long retrospective narrative of fabulous adventures once he had returned, would have been out of place and out of character since the whole mood of the poem changes with the arrival in Ithaca, where all is concentrated upon the pressing and immediate concerns of the present.

Disguise and dénouement

Odysseus arrives in Ithaca at night by way of the magic ship of the Phaeacians who then silently depart, leaving him alone sleeping upon the shore. Homer has been much criticised here on the grounds of improbability. Do not the demands of realism require that the hero be awake at the great moment of return? Homer uses this particular fiction, which he narrates very briefly, to satisfy the demands of the plot that Odysseus arrive unheralded and unheeded in his own country. Secrecy is necessary for him not only if he is to succeed in the plot against the suitors but simply if he is to save his own skin. As he remarks to Athene, without her aid he would have met the same end as Agamemnon (XIII, 383–5). But the device of the landing is brilliantly exploited by Homer for ironic effect. When he wakes up, Odysseus fails in the mist to recognise his native home and imagines that the Phaeacians have played him a trick in abandoning him in a foreign land. Athene appears on the scene disguised as a young shepherd to reveal the truth to him. He then tells the first of his false Cretan tales, keeping his identity secret. When the goddess declares herself she tells him the lie of the land, devises a disguise for him and sets him off to see his faithful servant Eumaeus. In this instance the irony works against Odysseus, and he reveals his cautious and crafty nature in inventing the Cretan tale. In the encounter with Athene, Odysseus proves himself to be the arch-schemer and worthy recipient of Athene's advice and encouragement. Subsequently, when Odysseus is disguised and un-known, the irony works against the rest of the characters who each in turn are tested to reveal their true nature to Odysseus.

The narrative art of Homer is manifest in the skill with which he uses the disguise of Odysseus, both as a realistic device in a credible plot and as a means of sustaining maximum human interest in his story through ironic effect. Odysseus reveals himself only when absolutely necessary and only to those who are to help him in the suitor-slaying. This is the plan and it is jeopardised only when the old nurse Eurycleia almost gives the game away by telling Penelope. The disguise is the means by which Odysseus tests loyalties and finds out for himself at first hand what is actually happening in Ithaca. But Homer's strategy is to enrich his plot with as many recognition scenes as possible. The first occurs when Odysseus recognises Ithaca and then the goddess in disguise (XIII). Then comes the recognition of father and son (XVI), followed by recognition of master and faithful dog (XVII), master and old nurse (XIX), master and faithful retainer (XXII), the climactic recognition of husband and wife (XXII), and finally the recognition of son and father (XXIV). We can see that it might well be expedient for Odysseus to keep Penelope in the dark, but of course Homer wants the great recognition scene between husband and wife to be delayed to a point at which it has maximum effect. All these recognition scenes are full of pathos and psychological interest. The three most poignant naturally involve Odysseus in his closest relations. Through them Homer cele-brates the most basic natural bonds of human life between parent and child and, above all, between husband and wife.

Through the disguise Homer makes Odysseus experience at first hand the sufferings endured by his household and the iniquities perpe-trated by the suitors. Our sympathies are firmly enlisted on the side of the hero and against the suitors with every insult and injury he suffers, so that in the richly deserved punishment of the suitors the interests of poetic justice are firmly upheld. Hence the disguise is used by Homer as a moral test. Not only do characters prove loyal and steadfast to Odys-seus but in their compassionate treatment of the apparently destitute stranger, Eumaeus, Telemachus and Penelope (unlike the suitors) prove themselves loyal to the highest moral standards of Homeric civil-isation, so that the disguise comes to be the means through which the underlying morality of the poem is most effectively revealed. The dis-guise can therefore be said to fulfil three functions simultaneously. The first is strategic in the plot to kill the suitors, the second is psychologi-cal in the reaction of the characters in the recognition scenes, and the third is moral in the definition and test of character and behaviour.

The character of Eumaeus is revealed in his civilised respect for the indigent beggar. His treatment of the stranger is a humble version of that accorded to Odysseus in Scherie and to Telemachus in Pylos and Sparta. Not only is the character of the humble Eumaeus exalted, we also have a new view of Odysseus as the good master. There are many poignant ironies in their encounter, not least when Eumaeus believes the Cretan tale told by Odysseus but disbelieves the oath that Odysseus will shortly return to set his house in order. This leads Eumaeus to tell the tale of the Aetolian stranger who came with assurances of Odysseus's imminent return (XIV, 378–89). Those expecting Odysseus have been fooled before so that their disbelief is well founded. In this detail, as in others, Homer is careful to make the reactions of his characters spring from credible motives true to their experience. During his time with Eumaeus, Odysseus learns first hand from a human source what is happening in his kingdom and is able to test his continuing loyalty which will be needed in the critical encounter. Having so far advanced his plot, Homer weaves together the double strands by arranging for the speedy return home of Telemachus. Details of his journey are described with brevity since the focus is now upon Odysseus in Ithaca.

That Telemachus should stop at Eumaeus's hut on his return is entirely natural given the danger to his life, so that the scene is set for the first great recognition scene between father and son. Before then in his treatment of the unknown stranger Telemachus, like Eumaeus, reveals his piety and good nature. Odysseus sees how his absence has affected his son and how his son longs for his return. The plot takes a natural advance when Telemachus sends Eumaeus to the palace to let Penelope know of his safe return. When Odysseus reveals himself, Telemachus at first expresses disbelief thinking he must be a god. Together they then secretly plot the destruction of their enemies. Meanwhile the suitors publicly discuss the return of Telemachus who has evaded their ambush at sea. Antinous recommends that he be killed before he returns to the palace. They dare not kill him openly because of fear of public opinion. This new detail is given here to add credibility to the story. The speech of Antinous (XVI, 364–92) also declares his intention that Telemachus's lands be seized and divided between them. The suitors' plot is a vivid reminder of the rottenness in the state of Ithaca. The issues of Homer's plot are now starkly clear; good is ranged against bad, the few are ranged against the many. The triumph of right can only be accomplished by a strategy of controlled cunning.

The action now moves naturally to the palace with the return first of Telemachus and then of Odysseus, who arrives separately lest he arouse suspicion or questions concerning his relation with Telemachus. He suffers the first of many indignities when the goatherd Melantheus, a foil to Eumaeus, insults him and kicks him on the way to the palace. Odysseus plays the role of beggar in his own house to see with his own eyes exactly what is going on, further to test character and motive and

to wait for his opportunity. Homer uses the disguise for ironic and
pathetic effect as before, but also, through the indignities heaped upon
him, to increase our sympathy for Odysseus in his righteous anger, and
further, to tarnish the suitors, thus making his vengeance seem entirely
justified. Once in the palace Odysseus confronts the suitors, all of
whom give him alms with the exception of Antinous who throws a stool
at him (XVII, 462–5). He then has to compete with the resident beggar
Irus, much to the amusement of the suitors. After the fight he warns
Amphinomus of the fate awaiting those who disregard the laws, and
Amphinomus is filled with foreboding of disaster (XVIII, 125–57).
The warning and its effect are included to mitigate the sudden horror
of the punishment that is to be visited upon the suitors. They have been
warned. Later Eurymachus mocks and insults Odysseus, and when he
replies in kind, Eurymachus throws a stool at him (XVIII, 394). Odys-
seus is insulted by some of the maidservants (XVIII, 321) and by
another of the suitors, Ctesippus, who throws a cow's hoof at him
(XX, 299). He witnesses the waste of his resources as the servants pre-
pare a whole day's feasting for the festival of Apollo. Not all the
behaviour of the suitors is equally outrageous. There is displeasure at
Antinous's refusal to give alms, for example, and another of the suit-
ors called Agelaus makes a conciliatory speech full of good sense after
Telemachus has complained of their treatment of the beggar (XX,
322–37). That Homer's villains should be susceptible to better feelings
and right behaviour is a further example of his skill as a storyteller
since their better moments serve only to emphasise the violation of
Greek manners represented by their general behaviour. Despite the
speech of Agelaus, the description of their last supper concludes with
laughter and raillery at the beggar's expense.

Odysseus's entanglement with the suitors is spread over four books
(XVII–XX). Enclosed within it are his conversations with Penelope,
the recognition by Eurycleia and the momentous decision of Penelope
to arrange for the contest with the bow, the device by which the plot is
advanced and unravelled. In a speech she makes to the suitors in Odys-
seus's presence (XVIII, 251–80) Penelope reveals her loyalty to Odys-
seus, the suffering she has endured in his absence and the crisis she is
facing now that Telemachus has grown up. She recalls his precise
instructions that if he had not returned from Troy by the time that their
son grew a beard she should marry the man of her choice and leave the
palace. Odysseus sees for himself not only that his wife is loyal but that
she is fulfilling his every instruction. To his delight she demands that
the suitors woo in the customary way, with presents. Antinous agrees
to this but also says that they will not leave the palace till she chooses
one of their number. Odysseus sees for himself her response to the
dilemma she faces. In her treatment of the destitute stranger, like

Eumaeus and Telemachus, Penelope shows her essential good nature and her delicate feeling for propriety. Their long conversation, interrupted by the recognition scene involving Eurycleia, and centred upon the absent husband actually present, is full of irony and pathos. Penelope weeps for her absent husband, Odysseus silently grieves for his sorrowing wife. Unburdening her soul to the stranger, she tells him of the stratagem of the web and of the desire of her parents, as well as Telemachus, that she remarry. The audience feel the weight of pressure upon her as she draws towards her decision. Without revealing himself Odysseus tries to offer her comfort with his Cretan tale in which he claims to have met Odysseus and with his assurance that he will return. Penelope remains unconvinced (XIX, 312–16), and her scepticism echoes that of Eumaeus and Telemachus. In what is a clear manoeuvre Odysseus arranges to be washed by his old nurse Eurycleia. She, too, is to be put to the test, for there is a role for her in the final denouement. Renewing their conversation, Penelope tells the stranger of her indecision. Is she to stay put or go with the best of the suitors? Now that Telemachus has grown up she is faced with his desire that she should go so that the estate will not be eaten up. She then tells the stranger of a dream which he interprets as an indication that Odysseus will soon return to slay the suitors. Penelope, however, has little faith in dreams, and announces her decision to propose a trial of strength with the bow. That she should come to this decision in conversation with Odysseus is powerfully ironic.

In the preliminaries to the final reckoning Homer is careful to be as realistic as possible within the restrictions imposed upon him by the story of the bow. There is a deliberate strategy. At the last minute Odysseus reveals his identity to Eumaeus and Philoetius so that he and Telemachus have allies in the fight. The suitors' arms are removed. Decencies are observed when Penelope and the women are withdrawn from the scene before the slaughter. Telemachus nearly manages to string the bow thus proving his worth, but Odysseus intervenes to prevent him, for were he to succeed the plan would misfire. He examines the bow carefully himself while Eurycleia and Philoetius bar the doors to the women's quarters and to the courtyard. So surprised are the suitors when Antinous their leader is killed that they believe his death to be accidental until Odysseus reveals himself. Thereupon Eurymachus, asking for mercy, blames Antinous and in so doing admits to the justice of Odysseus's anger, confessing without defence to the misdeeds committed in Odysseus's house. He blames Antinous for the plot against Telemachus, saying that he aimed to make himself king of Ithaca (XXII, 45–59). It is natural that Eurymachus should shift blame to the suitors' ringleader, but Homer had earlier specifically implicated Eurymachus in the plot against Telemachus (XVI, 448). The confession is strategically placed. Homer has seen to it that the suitors are defence-less both literally and morally. Odysseus's vengeance is therefore poet-ically just. As avenger he is without mercy and even goes to the extent of hanging the maids who had taken the part of the suitors. The fight itself is complicated when the suitors manage to gain access to arms. This has the effect of casting Odysseus and his friends in a more heroic light: they do not simply slaughter unarmed men. Finally Odysseus orders Eurycleia to fumigate the hall with sulphur, so that the house is finally cleansed.

The two final books are concerned primarily with the emotional reunion between husband and wife and between father and son, but the action is not at a standstill. There is a possibility of vengeance on the part of the relations of the suitors and this issue is not in fact settled until the final lines of the poem so that the momentum of the story is maintained to the last. The details of the recognition scene have been well prepared. The caution and scepticism of Penelope are intensifica-tions of the previous reactions of Eumaeus and Telemachus, despite the latter's impatient rebuke of his mother. Penelope's desire to be sure complements the need of Odysseus to see for himself how things are. The interview between them is interrupted by Odysseus's practical measures to delay news of what has happened from reaching the out-side world. When they talk again Penelope has recollected herself and tests Odysseus. When she finally yields she compares her position to that of Helen thus crystallising for the audience the prudence of her character by contrast (XXIII, 218–24). Odysseus tells her of his wan-derings but Homer is brief, for they are not to the point at this stage of his plot. The mention of Calypso's promises of immortality and ageless youth is well placed, suggesting that Penelope's faithfulness has its counterpart in a corresponding loyalty in Odysseus.

In the final book the scene shifts to the underworld whither Hermes is ushering the souls of the suitors. The discourse of Achilles and Aga-memnon contrasts the heroic death of the former with the appalling murder of the latter, both of which fates are implicitly contrasted with the happier fate of Odysseus. The suitors tell their version of their mis-erable end, whereupon Agamemnon sets the seal of heroic approval upon Odysseus's action and makes the inevitable comparison between Penelope and Clytemnestra. Odysseus sees for himself the distress of his father before revealing himself to Laertes with whom he discusses the present difficulty. When news of the death of the suitors is spread abroad an assembly is called in which opinion is divided. But the cry for vengeance is heeded, so that Odysseus and Telemachus face the Ithacan opposition until Athene commands the peace with which the poem concludes.

Until the last lines of the poem the re-establishment of Odysseus as master of his own house cannot be said to be secure. The last lines, consequently, leave us with a satisfying sense of completeness; the end to which Homer has been working from the beginning has now been reached.

The divine machinery

Homer's manipulation of his 'divine machinery' serves to clarify the main outline of the plot so that the audience are free to concentrate not so much upon what will happen next but upon how it will happen. As to what will happen the ultimate issue is never in doubt. Athene in the disguise of Mentor predicts the suitors' doom at the end of Book II. The audience are told the story; the surprise and suspense are related not to the ultimate outcome but to the manner in which it is brought about. Through the utterances and interventions of the gods the audience see the human action from an Olympian point of view.

A council of the gods is a convenient way of setting the poem in motion. Athene rebukes Zeus for hostility to Odysseus. Zeus protests in reply that it is Poseidon who hates Odysseus because he had blinded his son Polyphemus the Cyclops. As Zeus expresses no objection to the homecoming of Odysseus, Athene proposes to send Hermes to Ogygia to free him and to send Telemachus to Sparta and Pylos to look for Odysseus, an enterprise that will redound to his credit. From Nestor Telemachus learns of the hostility of Athene to the returning Greeks. In the council of the gods in Book V Zeus despatches Hermes to Ogygia telling the exact course of his twenty day journey to Scherie and the circumstances of his return in a brief summary of the action from Books V to XIII. In Book XIII Athene arranges the disguise of Odysseus and helps plan the destruction of the suitors in which she promises to take part. In the fight she appears with her aegis. In the final lines of the poem Zeus and Athene, like the 'deus ex machina' in Greek tragedy, solve the problem of continuing resistance to Odysseus by intervening to prevent further bloodshed.

In every human action the gods are involved. Athene guards and guides Telemachus. She sends a phantom sister to comfort Penelope. She puts the idea for the expedition to wash clothes in Nausicaa's head and enshrouds Odysseus in mist as he makes his way to the palace. The divine presence magnifies the protagonists but it also identifies the gods with the cause of Odysseus, as do the various divine signs apparent in the poem. In the first Ithacan council Zeus sends an omen which the soothsayer interprets as spelling doom to the suitors. Through the prophecy of the soothsayer Homer gives a brief summary of the whole of his plot. Just before the final reckoning Odysseus prays to Zeus to send a sign if it is true that he has been guided on his homeward journey by the gods. Zeus obligingly thunders in a cloudless sky. This follows Penelope's account of the dream in which an eagle destroys a flock of geese which has clear reference to the destruction of the suitors by Odysseus. Penelope mistrusts the dream but the audience know better. Dreams, divine signs and prophecies are all used by Homer to give shape to his narrative and to propel it forward, to heighten tension, and to suggest an underlying fate, unseen but inevitable, gradually being brought to fruition in the outcome of the action.

The well-made plot

From a review of the way in which Homer has managed the action, it is now possible to point to a number of conclusions concerning the artistry of Homer in the construction of the *Odyssey*. He tells us much of the story of Odysseus and perpetuates his fame as a great traveller and wanderer, but the great skill of Homer is revealed in the most obvious feature of the structure, in his beginning in the middle of things ('in medias res'). In fact it could be said that like the writers of Greek tragedy who followed him he begins near the end of things, at a point in the story just before the grand climax of events or what the Greeks called the catastrophe. Although the word is always associated with calamity in English, in Greek catastrophe simply implies a great reversal of fortune such as we have in the *Odyssey*, where it is a reversal from adversity to prosperity brought about by the killing of the suitors in Book XXII. Homer has therefore deliberately departed from the natural chronological order of events. When he gives an account of himself to Penelope, Odysseus in his summary of what has happened to him since the fall of Troy begins with his victory over the Cicones (narrated to the Phaeacians in Book X). Homer begins near the end of things at a point of high tension, at a decisive moment for Odysseus and a critical juncture for his Ithacan household. The main action comprising the homecoming and re-establishment of Odysseus in Ithaca takes place in a concentrated period of time amounting to little more than forty days in the life of Odysseus. The rest of his nine years away from home after the fall of Troy is accounted for in a retrospective narrative that is well connected but rigorously subordinate to the main action. This artificial order enables Homer to achieve maximum concentration and unity.

In his famous analysis of tragedy in the *Poetics*, the philosopher and critic Aristotle (384–322BC) also makes incidental remarks about epic* and he commends the Homeric epics expressly for their unity of action. Aristotle makes the point that a plot does not have unity because it

* See particularly *Poetics* VII, VIII, XVII, XXIII, and XXIV.

deals with a single hero. Many things happen to an individual which do not necessarily make up a unity, and, at the same time, an individual may be concerned in many actions that cannot be combined into one action (*mia praxis*). Homer, he says, whether through knowledge of his craft (*techne*) or through a natural instinct (*physis*) knew this and did not put into his *Odyssey* all that happened to Odysseus but constructed the *Odyssey* around a single action in which all the parts are connected and cohere. This is the classical conception of a well-made plot and it is classically embodied in the *Iliad* and the *Odyssey*. To discuss Homer in terms of Aristotle may serve to clarify essential features of the classical epic form found in Homer. The philosopher's principles and ideas are a logical and analytical expression of characteristic aesthetic tendencies first evidenced in the Homeric poems and through them permeating all aspects of Greek life. It is no exaggeration to say that Aristotle only thought as he did because of the shaping influence of Homer upon Greek art.

The *Odyssey* in Aristotle's formulation is the representation of an action that is whole, complete and of a certain magnitude. A whole is that which has a beginning, a middle and an end. Because of the contraction of time the beginning, middle and end of the *Odyssey* do not follow a straightforward chronological sequence as is the case with the *Iliad*; the beginning and the middle are involved in one another. But in the essential sense the complication at the beginning of the action is subject to a natural development until the climax and the dénouement. Magnitude in the literal sense is the virtue by which the epic form is recognised. Aristotle remarks that the essence of the *Odyssey* – what he calls the *logos*, which we might translate as the irreducible story – is quite short. The greater scale and length of an epic is achieved through the inclusion of episodes. But in the case of tragedy, Aristotle uses the word magnitude in a different sense to mean the right kind of length to allow a change of fortune in a sequence of events that follow one another either inevitably or according to probability.

In the change of fortune in the *Odyssey* there is a double issue: prosperity for the good characters and adversity for the bad. The issue is more characteristic of comedy than tragedy. The sequence of events should be natural; there should be nothing inexplicable (Aristotle's word is *alogos*, akin to illogical). Only a great poet like Homer can conceal an absurdity like the landing of Odysseus in Ithaca (he is deposited at night asleep on the shore by the Phaeacians who abruptly leave). But it will be objected, how can the sequence of events in the *Odyssey* be natural when it is brought about by a supernatural agency? When the goddess of wisdom advises Telemachus to go and search for his father, we may regard the goddess as cause and instigator with her own reasons for promoting the action. These reasons can be part of the overall chain of cause and effect. Or we may feel that this is Homer's way of arranging for Telemachus to make a decision to go for himself. In the main action, free will in the human sphere is not incompatible with divine aid which is generally of a different character from the use of magic (as in the case of the moly (or magical herb) given to Odysseus in the Circe episode). In any event the marvellous can be more readily accommodated in epic, because it is narrative, than in a tragedy which has to be represented on the stage.

The sequence of events in the *Odyssey* is natural in terms of cause and effect in the human sphere (the all too human gods have their own motives and reasons for acting) but it is also well connected and easy in an artistic sense. One of the distinguishing excellencies of Homer is his art of connection and transition. This is surely true even in the instance in which he has been criticised. That Odysseus should wake up after his fabulous narrative and after his fabulous journey in a mist-shrouded Ithaca which he is unable to recognise at first, is a masterly transition which marks the emergence of the hero into a new and different order of reality.

The sequence of events is made easy by the masterly use of setting. Unity of action and concentration of time are not matched in the *Odyssey* as they are in the *Iliad* by a corresponding unity of place. The action begins and ends in Ithaca but it also takes us with Telemachus to Pylos and Sparta, then back to Odysseus in Ogygia and with the hero from there to Scherie, before the final return to Ithaca. Variety of place and scene is a natural consequence of Homer's point of departure. Unity here is achieved through the continuous presence of one or other of the two protagonists of the double-stranded plot whose fortunes we are following. But there is also a deeper unity in the appropriateness of setting with mood, action, theme and tale pervasive throughout. Most obviously Phaeacia is the ideal setting for the fabulous tales of Odysseus's wanderings. In Ithaca an altogther different spirit prevails. The Cretan tales of Odysseus are of a different and less fabulous kind from those in the first half of the poem. As we move from Ithaca to Pylos and Sparta and then to Ogygia and Scherie and then back to Ithaca, the whole character of the poem changes so that the physical movement is part of a larger movement in which the structure of the poem is revealed.

In the arrangement of the incidents (structure: the Greek word is *systasis* which is from the same root as syntax, drawing together) Aristotle remarked that the various parts should not only be arranged in an orderly way but also have a certain magnitude of their own. For beauty consists in magnitude (*megathos*) and orderly arrangement (*taxis*). The beauty of the *Odyssey* as a structure derives from its unity and from the way in which the parts that constitute that unity are all well-proportioned, having a proper magnitude in relation to one another. Here proportion must also involve the connection of the parts, the pacing of the poem and the management of climax. In a good structure the component parts must be so arranged that nothing can be transposed or removed without dislocating and damaging the unity of the whole. Most readers would agree that the *Odyssey* meets this requirement in a way that, for example, the larger version of *Dr Faustus* by the English dramatist Christopher Marlowe (1564−93), which includes all the comic scenes, does not.

We can best be made aware of the proportion of the poem by trying to envisage a different structure. If Odysseus had told his adventures at length to Penelope after the recognition scene, this would clearly have thrown the whole poem off balance. As it is, just a summary here of the adventures is judicious. If Homer had developed the return journey of Telemachus, or the relationship between Odysseus and Calypso, such developments would have meant further imbalance and the inclusion of material extraneous to the main action at times when the progressive movement of the poem demands that the action be advanced. Whether through knowledge of his craft or some divine natural instinct, Homer knew when to be brief and to use summary, and when to be expansive in the creation of vivid scenes such as the moments of recognition in the second half. With regard to the pacing of events, the arrival in Ithaca after Odysseus has been raised in the audience's imagination through the Phaeacian narrative and at a point midway through the poem, is surely judicious timing. The gradual build-up to the final climax is finely managed. The increasing pressure on Penelope interacts with the plot against Telemachus and the malevolence of the suitors towards Odysseus in disguise. All is intensified by the inclusion of omens, dreams and prophecies. Economy must be an aspect of proportion, and there is conspicuous economy in the use of the bow as a device both for Penelope to test the suitors and for Odysseus to kill them. In other versions of the homecoming, Odysseus took Penelope into his confidence, but Homer chooses to end his poem not solely with just revenge and bloodshed but in a double climax involving the more human emotional recognition scenes, so that even after the climax of the physical action the poem is propelled forward to a second climax for which there has been a steadily rising expectation.

The plot of the *Odyssey* is essentially simple and clear; the broad outlines are easily grasped. The overall simplicity and clarity of design which are suggested in this discussion of the plot of the Homeric *Odyssey* can be readily appreciated if the classic original is compared with the modern novel alluding to it, *Ulysses* (1922) by James Joyce (1882−1941). Yet the overall simplicity does not altogether exclude complexity. Comparing the two poems, Aristotle remarked that while the *Iliad* has a simple plot turning upon calamity, the *Odyssey* has a complex plot and turns on character. In parenthesis he cites the many recognition scenes as a facet of Odyssean complexity. To the complication of the unravelling of the plot brought about by the varied use of disguise, Aristotle might have added, if he had wished to drive his point home, the two other major sources of Odyssean complexity discussed above, namely the point of departure 'in medias res' with the use of retrospective narrative and the complication of the double stranded plot. Just as simplicity does not exclude complexity, so the unity of the *Odyssey* is not bought at the expense of variety. Pylos and Sparta, Ogygia and Scherie, and Ithaca all represent distinct worlds and phases within the poem. Yet what might be regarded as the potentially discordant elements of romance and realistic fiction are harmoniously blended through skilful use of setting and mastery of transition. That the *Odyssey* has been variously called an adventure story, a moral tale, the precursor of romance or of picaresque fiction, or simply the first realistic novel, indicates the variety of interests which it can satisfy and the rich and varied texture of the poem.

Character

In his analysis of tragedy, Aristotle calls the plot the soul of the play, arguing that a tragedy without characterisation is possible while one without action is not. Epic is a different form, of course, and Aristotle specifically remarks that a distinguishing feature of the *Odyssey* is that its action turns upon character. Aristotle's argument that character is a function subordinate to the main action, serves as a useful reminder that an artist will develop a character to serve a purpose in the work of art rather than create a work of art to delineate character.

The purely functional character is exemplified in the person of Mentor who has given his name to what he represents in the *Odyssey*, an experienced guardian or guide. All the characters have a clear function in relation to the main action. Odysseus is the just and responsible king who is to restore order to Ithaca on his return. Around him we can see the dutiful son, the loyal wife, the faithful retainer and the good old nurse, and in opposition to him the wicked suitors. But the *Odyssey* would have been a very flat tale if this were all. Homer has given the world a gallery of fully-rounded characters who have an imaginative appeal that transcends the poem in which they occur. This is particularly true of Odysseus himself who has exerted a fascination on subsequent readers comparable to that of Shakespeare's Hamlet. To a large extent this is a consequence of his dramatic presentation; characters are established not by authorial pronouncement but by their own words and deeds.

The suitors

The suitors, like the companions of Odysseus, are constantly referred to en masse. As the companions of Odysseus take no part in the main action Homer does not concern himself with their characterisation. But in the case of the suitors he has carefully distinguished three quite different forms of iniquity.

Antinous their leader, whose very name suggests one who is antagonistic (compared with Alcinous's name which suggests strength of mind), is straightforwardly a nasty piece of work. All his speeches are direct, insulting and without disguise. As leader of the gang he initiates the plot against Telemachus in the beginning and renews it later when it has misfired. He angrily insults the disguised Odysseus and refuses to give him food when he begs for it, throwing a footstool at him instead. For this gross breach of the sacred Greek custom of hospitality he is rebuked even by his fellow suitors. Through him Homer represents the suitors' behaviour in its ugliest aspect. All his speeches and actions point to this end.

Eurymachus seems altogether a more genial fellow. In contrast to the anger and emotion of Antinous, he makes a soothing speech to Telemachus at the opening, assuring him of their good intentions (I, 400−11). In the council, though he is stern with the soothsayer, he nevertheless does not blame Penelope at length as Antinous does, but puts more emphasis upon the apparently reasonable solution that Telemachus should send Penelope back to her father's house (II, 194−207). Homer in the beginning does not implicate him directly by name in the plot against Telemachus. Later we hear that he is the favoured choice of Penelope's father and brothers (XV, 17). Telemachus even advises Theoclymenus to go to Eurymachus's house where he can expect to meet a more orderly reception than in his own home (XV, 518). When Penelope rebukes the suitors for plotting against her son, it is Eurymachus who makes a soothing speech assuring her of his protection for her son whom he regards as the dearest of men. He speaks to encourage her (and to gain her good opinion) 'while plotting her son's death' (XVI, 448). Later he flatters Penelope, praising her beauty when she appears before the suitors to elicit gifts from them (XVIII, 245−9). While Antinous exhibited simple anger at the beggar, Eurymachus at first makes jokes about his baldness and ugliness to ridicule him and is only driven to anger and the use of a footstool when Odysseus has provoked him in return. When Odysseus finally reveals himself Eurymachus admits the suitors' iniquities and tries to shift all the blame onto Antinous. All in all he is a more subtle character than Antinous, with a more attractive exterior masking hidden cunning. His iniquity is more hypocritical and disguised.

Amphinomus, Penelope's favourite among the suitors, who still has some goodness at heart (XVI, 397–8), recognises the iniquity of the plot against Telemachus when it has miscarried and diverts the suitors' thoughts away from further action (XVI, 400–5). He greets the beggar at the feast and wishes him good fortune. When the disguised Odysseus issues his warning, he is heavy at heart and filled with foreboding (XVIII, 153–5). His guilt, in contrast to the insensitivity of Antinous or the hypocrisy of Eurymachus, is strongly felt in this scene. After Eurymachus has been provoked to throw a stool at Odysseus Amphinomus urges reverence towards Telemachus's guest and makes the peace (XVIII, 412–21). Nevertheless it is his doom, pronounced by Athene (XVIII, 155–6), to die alongside the rest. Homer leaves us to draw our own conclusions.

The character of Antinous is constant throughout the action, that of Eurymachus is gradually revealed by the action, and that of Amphinomus is introduced at a moment in the action when the issue of guilt comes to the fore. These three characters are clearly differentiated in a realistic way that is quite consistent in each individual case. Their reactions and behaviour together are varied and make up an interesting pattern of diversity credible within the group. This is a source of great human interest in the plot; the suitors are not mere ciphers. Furthermore, however simple the broad moral outline of the poem may be, the suitors are allowed a point of view. In the initial speech to the assembly in which Antinous puts all the blame on Penelope for promising one thing and performing another, there is some justice. The whole situation has the complexity of real life particularly when, as a result of the point of departure 'in medias res,' there is some difficulty in unravelling the threads of the knotty problem that Homer has presented us with at the beginning of the poem.

Telemachus

In the case of Telemachus the initial course of the action is grounded in his self-assertion now that he has come of age. The self-assertion is what finally causes Penelope to initiate the contest with the bow. Odysseus had told her to leave his house and marry again (if he had not returned) when their son had grown a beard on his chin (XVIII, 251–80). It is not the physical fact of his coming of age that moves Penelope but the proof that he is now becoming a power in his own right. At the beginning of the poem when she complains about Phemius's song Telemachus orders her to go to her chamber whereupon she shows great surprise (I, 345–61). The motif is repeated later when he tells his mother that he will give the bow to whom he wishes, and bids her retire (XXI, 344–55). The suitors are similarly surprised by his speeches in the assembly which he has called, by his ability to bring off the proposed journey and by his sternness towards them when he has returned to the palace. At the opening of the poem Athene, in disguise, admonishes Telemachus that few sons are worthy of their fathers; Orestes is held up as an example of a son who well served the interests of his father (I, 296–302; II, 276–8). In the course of the poem Telemachus is to prove himself worthy. He passes the various tests that are laid for him, and shows the self-control in the second half of the poem that he had not quite managed earlier when he burst into tears in the assembly. He almost strings the bow, proves himself adept in the final encounter, and Laertes rejoices to see his son and grandson vying with each other in valour (XXIV, 513–15).

Odysseus

It is on the character of Odysseus that the action principally turns. The essence of his characterisation in Homer is simple and clear and is indicated in the various epithets given to him. In the opening line of the poem he is said to be *polytropos*, variously translated as the man of many ways, many turns or many parts. He is also *polymetis* and *polymechanos*, the man of much contrivance and many devices, and of course *polytlas*, much suffering and enduring. All four epithets are united by the prefix *poly* representing him as the man of great experience who has seen cities and known the minds of men. His knowledge of the world based on experience is matched by his experience of the world – he has done, achieved and suffered many things – from which he has learned. The following conversation in a biography of James Joyce suggests something of the completeness of Odysseus:

'Your complete man in literature is, I suppose, Ulysses?'
'Yes,' said Joyce . . . 'you mentioned Hamlet. Hamlet is a human being, but he is a son only. Ulysses is son to Laertes, but he is father to Telemachus, husband to Penelope, lover of Calypso, companion in arms of the Greek warriors around Troy, and King of Ithaca. He was subjected to many trials, but with wisdom and courage came through them all . . . Another thing, the history of Ulysses did not come to an end when the Trojan War was over. It began just when the other Greek heroes went back to live the rest of their lives in peace. And then – ' Joyce laughed – 'he was the first gentleman in Europe. When he advanced, naked, to meet the young princess he hid from her maidenly eyes the parts that mattered of his brine-soaked, barnacle-encrusted body. He was an inventor too. The tank was his creation. Wooden horse or iron box – it doesn't matter. They are both shells containing armed warriors.'
'What do you mean,' said Budgen, 'by a complete man? For

example, if a sculptor makes a figure of a man then that man is all-round, three-dimensional, but not necessarily complete in the sense of being ideal. All human bodies are imperfect, limited in some way, human beings too. Now your Ulysses...'

'He is both,' said Joyce. 'I see him from all sides, and therefore he is all-round in the sense of your sculptor's figure. But he is a complete man as well – a good man.'*

Joyce emphasised that Odysseus was not a god, for he was not exempt from human fraility. He was not perfect, but decent.

Homer's polytropic hero and his polytropic plot reflect each other perfectly. Odysseus's character unfolds naturally with the action. His absence at the start creates a great expectation of him which is fuelled by the reminiscences of Nestor, Helen and Menelaus. In the plot these reminiscences also serve as anticipations. For Nestor, recalling the heroic enterprise of the campaign now long since past, Odysseus was the master strategist (III, 120). Nestor the sage old counsellor found in Odysseus a kindred spirit sharing his political sense. They never spoke at variance in the assembly of the Achaeans. Menelaus, a man of action himself, recalls the man of action who did more on behalf of the Greek cause at Troy than anyone else (IV, 106–7). Helen, herself a subtle figure, tells the story of the clever ruse through which Odysseus entered Troy disguised as a beggar, on a mission of intelligence (III, 240–56). Menelaus then tells of Odysseus's behaviour inside the Wooden Horse when he had the presence of mind to keep the Greeks from revealing themselves. He also comments on Odysseus's physical prowess in wrestling. These anticipations all help to raise a vivid idea of the polytropic hero in the audience's imagination.

On Calypso's isle Odysseus first enters the poem as the long suffering hero, alone and tearful. When Calypso tells him she will help him to leave, he mistrusts her, requiring a solemn oath that she is not plotting his ruin. The nymph is amused at the suspicious nature of Odysseus's crafty mind. In making the raft he shows himself to be practical, resourceful and a good craftsman. In the storm we see the heroic spirit of Odysseus recoiling from the horror of a death at sea, wishing instead that like Achilles he could have died on the plains of Troy, a death that would have spread his fame abroad. In the sea Homer shows him to be constantly using his wits to extricate himself from trouble. Once on land he collects himself and in his interview with Nausicaa shows a tact and delicacy of feeling that puts him in an altogether new light. His concern for her reputation is sensitive and civilised. At the palace his tact in dealing with the Phaeacians is politic but also decent in itself. When provoked he proves his physical excellence in the games. Declaring his

* Richard Ellmann, *James Joyce*, Oxford University Press, New York, 1959, pp.448–9.

identity at the opening of his retrospective narrative he announces that he is known among men for all manner of stratagems: his fame reaches the heavens (IX, 19). The word always associated with him and which he uses here is *dolos*: wiles, craft, stratagem, cunning. The account of his adventures reveals him to be the wily Greek who has been tested in a wide variety of experiences. When he has landed in Ithaca, he craftily invents his first Cretan tale to conceal his identity from the young shepherd who is Athene in disguise. When the goddess reveals herself she is amused at his cunning and inventiveness and his delight in lying tales. He does not immediately trust her, suspecting that she is beguiling him. Athene finds this very much in character, a character to which she is akin herself. She call him *epetes, agkinoos* and *echephron* (XIII, 332). These words all refer to qualities of mind. The first seems related to *epos* (word) and is variously translated as soft or fluent of speech or civilised; Odysseus certainly has a way with words. The second is intelligent or of quick understanding; he is always quick to sum up a situation and to grasp an opportunity. The third is having understanding, self-possessed, controlled, prudent; he generally shows great presence of mind. It is striking that this characterisation comes after these qualities have been fully demonstrated in the action and that it is put in the mouth of another character rather than delivered through direct authorial comment. These are the qualities of mind and character by virtue of which Odysseus has succeeded so far and they will be necessary if he is to succeed in repossessing his own house.

The rest of the plot is a test and display of these aspects of the hero's character. It shows his supreme *dolos*. His inventiveness is apparent in his devising credible tales which are always well adapted to the speaker and his audience. His quickness of mind is apparent throughout as he takes advantage of every opportunity, particularly in the way he encourages Penelope to arrange for the contest with the bow. As a strategist he is cautious, testing character and planning in advance as when he removes the armour from the hall. His self-control is evident in the way in which he sustains the disguise without giving himself away before he judges it to be expeditious either to those loyal to him or to his enemies. All of this requires that he be a consummate actor, confident in his role and adequate to all aspects of the situation confronting him – the true polytropic hero.

That Odysseus emerges as all-round and three dimensional in the words of James Joyce is a consequence of the way in which he is presented in Homer. It is not only that we see him in the many different roles that a man may be called upon to play – father, husband, son, master, lover, comrade-in-arms, politician, avenger, the list is a long one – but we also see him from many different points of view. Each point of view has ground for support in the action itself. His mother

Anticleia, for example, singles out his gentleness, and this aspect of his character (which does not exclude its opposite, for Odysseus can be stern and fierce) is evident in his dealings with Nausicaa and in the sensitivity shown to Penelope in the latter part of the poem. Homer even allows a critical view. To Eurylochus, Odysseus's adventures with the Cyclops and Circe illustrate his reckless disregard for the safety of his companions (X, 431–7). Different aspects of his character, overlapping and shading into one another but with a distinctly individual point of view, are given in the varied testimonies of Nestor, Helen, Menelaus, Anticleia, Athene, Penelope, Eumaeus, Eurycleia and Laertes. At the same time these testimonies tell something of the character of those who give them, so that they are only partial accounts, aspects and facets of the man as he appears to those who know him. As a result of this dramatic representation, the portrayal of Odysseus is multi-faceted and true to life. There is no one fixed stable point of view enforced by an omniscient narrator, with the exception of what is given in the epithets long-suffering and polytropic.

Odysseus appears to be a true-to-life character because of the perspective adopted upon his life in the form of the poem itself. This perspective is the larger aspect of points of view discussed above. Homer concentrates upon about forty days in his life. Of his future we hear a brief prophecy from Tiresias, and his past is contained in many reminiscences going back as far as his early youth in the memories of Eurycleia and Laertes. The *Odyssey* has the breadth of a great chronicle but with none of its limitations and restrictions. We are allowed a telescopic view but from a fixed point of time. The *Odyssey* gives a representation of a vivid extended present, highlights of the past and a brief intimation of the future. This in itself is a satisfying and credible form in which to present the imitation of life since it is universal. This is how we all experience time in which it seems that we are always 'in medias res' or near the end of things. The *Odyssey* does not purport to tell us the whole truth about Odysseus but to present the significant truth of forty days of his experience. In spite of that we do have a broad and telescopic view of his character over a greater period of time. Homer has concentration and breadth in ideal proportions. In his modern novel *Ulysses*, James Joyce deals with eighteen hours in the life of a contemporary man. Such intense concentration puts that life under a microscope in such a way that we lose a sense of overall form and coherence because of the perspective adopted. This perspective may be equally or more true to life. The simple point of contrast here is that Homer's perspective allows us to grasp the character and experience of Odysseus in some depth without losing coherence in detail. Homer presents life and character not in all its bewildering complexity but in a form in which we can see meaning and pattern.

Penelope

The character of Penelope is celebrated throughout the *Odyssey*. Her faithfulness and steadfastness are contrasted with Clytemnestra's disloyalty which proved to be the undoing of Agamemnon. In Hades the spirit of Agamemnon, after recounting the iniquity of his wife, tells Odysseus that there is no danger of his suffering a similar fate, as Penelope is too intelligent and understanding (XI, 444–6). In the final book the spirit of Agamemnon again pronounces judgement upon Penelope: 'Blessed is Odysseus in the great virtue of his wife, always loyal to him. The fame of her virtue (*arete*) will never perish, and the immortals will fashion a beautiful song in honour of Penelope the wise' (*echephron* – having understanding, prudent, self possessed: XXIV, 192–202). There is a fine decorum in this judgement. It acquires more authority from the lips of Agamemnon than if it had been delivered by Odysseus or by the narrator. (Indeed the whole Agamemnon story is woven into the *Odyssey* with great skill.) Odysseus's character is subtle and not without complexity given his role as the polytropic hero in a polytropic poem. But Penelope's virtue is pre-eminent and unequivocal. It is manifested in her constancy and suggested by the epithet given to her by Agamemnon and repeated throughout the poem. Nevertheless she is not a flat character. She is most sensitively presented; we see her suffering spirit under threat and always on the defensive. She has used her wits, and successfully outwitted the suitors for three years with the stratagem of the web. Faced with the stranger claiming to be Odysseus she is cautious and sceptical. Her caution has become proverbial. Telemachus thinks she is over-stubborn. She turns the tables on Odysseus and tests him with a stratagem of her own devising concerning their marriage bed. When she finally yields, she apologises to Odysseus, telling him of her fear that she might be deceived by a plausible stranger. She then calls to mind the example of Helen who, though she would never have slept with her foreign love if she could have foreseen the disastrous consequences of her action, nevertheless succumbed to a momentary infatuation (XXIII, 218–24). We may recall here Nestor's remark that Clytemnestra was a perfectly good woman until prevailed upon by her paramour (III, 265–6). Penelope's scepticism and caution are aspects of her intelligence and control. Given the dilemma in which she finds herself, they are perfectly reasonable and are elements of a credible psychological unity. The prominence of her virtue in the poem is one of the reasons (another is the prominence of Arete in the Phaeacian episode) that led the English Victorian writer Samuel Butler (1835–1902) to believe that the *Odyssey* had been composed by a woman.

Supporting roles

The role of Eumaeus, the good and faithful steward, is to afford shelter to Odysseus. He is straightforward, plainspeaking, pious and dutiful. In the humble setting of his hut, his frugal ways are contrasted with the arrogant profligacy of the suitors in the palace. In his entertainment of the indigent stranger he exhibits good sense, tolerance, sensitivity and tact that are indicative of true nobility, something that transcends position and fortune in life (Eumaeus is of noble origin). The good pigman is something of a moral touchstone and his role has some of the symbolic force of the good shepherd in the Christian story. He is, nevertheless, a fully realistic character very much associated with his setting and with the ordinary activities of his day-to-day life.

Similarly Eurycleia, the old nurse, is usually busy with the activities of housekeeping. She is made to serve a very different purpose. She is a good woman but her role has little symbolic force. Homer uses her memorably in the sequence of recognition scenes where her reaction of tumultuous enthusiasm (she upsets the washtub) almost gives the game away. Her cry of triumph after the suitor-slaying serves to make a moral point. It is not holy, says Odysseus, to exult over the deaths of the unworthy.

Laertes, a lonely and impotent figure of suffering in the absence of his son, is restored to active wellbeing in the final moments of the poem. Before Athene commands the peace, Odysseus exhorting Telemachus to do battle with the Ithacan opposition expresses confidence that he will not shame the house of their fathers which has always been foremost in valour and strength. As one of those fathers, Laertes rejoices in the competing strength of his son and grandson. In the joy of Laertes, the father figure, the regeneration of the house of Odysseus is thus completed.

While characters all have their individual parts to play within the action and their own particular behavioural traits to exhibit, integration is achieved through their subtle interaction and the ways they can be said to support one another. Crucial qualities of mind and character are reduplicated through a variety of parts. Athene remarks on the close natural affinity between herself and Odysseus. Like him she is a subtle spirit who delights in dissimulation and disguise. He is her favourite because he excels in the human sphere in all the qualities of mind and character for which she is known among the gods (XIII, 297–8). Odysseus is the master of wiles and trickery, but Penelope, in the stratagem of the web and in her test of Odysseus, exhibits a comparable guile and craft. Penelope's caution finds an echo in her husband's behaviour with Calypso and Athene, and as the beggar in disguise. In both cases it is an aspect of their good sense and control, as evidenced in the epithet *echephron* given to them both. Telemachus may be inexperienced but he is no fool and frequently merits the epithet *pepnumenos* – of sound understanding. When father and son plot the destruction of the suitors he gives good advice modifying his father's plans (XVI, 309–20). He has to use his wits and show self-control in his treatment of the suitors. In the crucial moment it is through his firm intervention that Odysseus is finally given the bow. He is conceived very much in his father's mould, and proves adequate to his supporting role because of qualities of character that he shares with his father. That characters should reinforce each other in this way lends realism and credibility to the plot. It also results in artistic cohesion. The qualities of mind and character which are vindicated in the action and through its outcome are manifested not only in the central character but are reinforced by their pervading presence in the poem as a whole.

Part 4

Hints for study

Homeric problems and questions

Underlying the account of the plot and characterisation in Part 3 is a conviction about the artistic excellence of the *Odyssey* and an assumption about its overall unity of design. But Homer has not been without his critics, and from earliest times adverse judgements have been made about aspects of his art. In antiquity books were produced of Homeric problems (Aristotle is said to have been the author of one such book) in which problems were raised and solutions discussed. Some of the problems and criticisms were niggling and silly, reflecting the philistinism of those who made them. Such hyper-criticism is associated with the name of Zoilus, a critic of Homer living in the fifth century BC. Others raised genuine problems which have since become part of the larger Homeric Question. What were earlier seen as artistic weaknesses or oddities have lately come to be regarded as points of evidence against unity of authorship in the argument of analytical critics. A representative selection of the commonest points that have been debated about the *Odyssey*, most but not all having a possible bearing upon the Homeric Question, and some of them of the niggling kind, is listed below in an order suggested by the arrangement of the poem itself.

(1) The relevance of much of what passes in Books I-IV (The Telemachid) has been questioned, as has the wisdom of Homer in delaying the appearance of his hero until Book V.
(2) Much depends upon the fact that Telemachus has just come of age. Eurynome remarks that he is now a 'bearded man' (XVIII, 176). Yet Odysseus has been away for twenty years, so that Telemachus must be over twenty.
(3) Does the folk motif of the web (first mentioned by Antinous at II, 96–122) violate the realistic spirit in which the events of Ithaca are represented?
(4) In comforting Penelope, why does not Athene reveal to her the whole truth (IV, 836–7)?
(5) Zeus declares that Odysseus must journey to Scherie without divine guidance (V, 32) yet Poseidon intervenes (V, 282) and Odysseus is helped by Ino, a water nymph (V, 351) and by Athene (V, 382).

(6) Odysseus covering himself with leaves is likened to a thrifty man on an outlying farm who keeps his fire alive under black ashes (V, 488–90). Does this simile demean the hero of the poem? Homer has been much criticised for his low images, particularly in similes. Earlier Odysseus had been likened to a cuttlefish (V, 432–3). The most notorious is the comparison of the restless state of the hero to a black pudding being tossed to and fro over a fire (XX, 25–7).

(7) Is Nausicaa immodest in saying that Odysseus is the sort of man she could marry? (VI, 244)

(8) Why does Odysseus fail to answer Arete's question about his identity? (VII, 238) Why is she given such prominence in the Phaeacian episode?

(9) What is the relevance and propriety of Demodocus's song about the illicit love of Ares and Aphrodite? (VIII, 266–366)

(10) Going ashore on the island of the Cyclopes, Odysseus decides to find out what sort of people live there, whether brutal or godfearing (IX, 175–6). He then has a foreboding that he is about to meet a being of enormous size (IX, 213–14). Is the episode well linked to the rest of the poem, or is the stitching whereby the folk tales of the deep sea yarns and the surrounding narrative are knitted together too obvious? Can the representation of Odysseus in the episodes as the man who desires to see things for himself be reconciled with the view we have of him in the main action as the hero who longs to return home?

(11) How just is the accusation of Eurylochus that Odysseus shows reckless folly in leading his men into dangers in which they lose their lives (X, 431–8)? If it is true, is it not damaging to the integrity of the hero either as a wise man or as one who is prudent and can be master of any situation?

(12) The eleventh book in its present form has been regarded either as a late interpolation in its entirety (is the overall design and effect of the poem impaired without it?) or as a later expansion of an original Homeric core. In Book VIII, Odysseus's instant departure is foretold (VIII, 150). In Book IX, he breaks off his narrative to announce that it is time to go to bed, and the Phaeacians press him to stay another day. This has been said to be a flimsy connection. Odysseus witnessed the death of Elpenor yet asks his spirit how he died. It has been argued that there are two conceptions of Hades. In the Minos scene (XI, 575 onwards) the ghosts appear to have their faculties intact whereas in the rest of the narrative they can only regain consciousness after drinking blood. Although Odysseus is above ground initially, it appears that he is actually in the underworld itself at points in the narrative when he is observing the activities of the ghosts. Not all that is described seems relevant to the poem. What is the point of the catalogue of women? What is the relevance of Elpenor and his fate?

(13) Homer has been censured on the grounds of implausibility for allowing Odysseus to be deposited in Ithaca asleep.

(14) The pace of the poem slackens in Book XIII. Not all readers have felt that the Ithacan narrative is well planned or well paced. Are all the stories told in Eumaeus's hut necessary, and, if so, is the narrative not too long? These scenes involving characters from low life have been thought more appropriate to comedy than to epic. In particular the device whereby Odysseus elicits a cloak from Eumaeus (XIV, 459–518), the encounter with Melantheus (XVII, 212–54), the fight with the beggar (XVIII, 1–116), the play on Irus's name (XVIII, 6), the various jokes and raillery of the suitors (for example, XVIII, 351–5 and XX, 292–8) have all been censured as violations of epic decorum.

(15) The character of Theoclymenus has puzzled commentators who have questioned his role in the poem. His history is given at length (XV, 223–56) yet he plays little effective part other than as an augur who foresees the death of the suitors (XX, 351–7).

(16) The episode involving the recognition of Odysseus by his dog Argus has been censured on the grounds of lowness (the mention of realistic details like the dunghill or the dog's fleas being a violation of epic dignity), improbability (the dog must have been over twenty years old with a very long memory) and sentimentality (XVII, 290–327).

(17) In a clear manoeuvre, Odysseus arranges that he should be washed by Eurycleia (XIX, 335–48). It then occurs to him that she might recognise him by the scar (XIX, 388–91). Is this bad strategy on the part of Odysseus and/or Homer? The long account of the incident in which Odysseus received the scar has been censured as a pointless digression (XIX 393–466).

(18) Penelope decides to institute the contest with the bow just at the moment when she has had a number of indications from different sources that Odysseus is about to return. Telemachus has told her that Odysseus is still alive (XVII, 142–6); both Theoclymenus (XVII, 152–61) and the stranger (XIX, 303–7) have prophesied his return. Is her decision adequately and credibly motivated?

(19) Is the killing of the suitors noble and heroic, brutal and primitive or just fanciful and incredible?

(20) There seems to be confusion in the plans to remove armour from the hall. Odysseus at XVI 281–98 tells Telemachus to remove all but two sets which are to be left in a handy position nearby. In the event Telemachus goes down to the storeroom where he picks out four sets (one each for their two helpers). What is to be made of this apparent contradiction? (XXII, 108–10)

(21) The punishment of the maids has been censured for being unnecessarily barbaric (XXII, 437–73).

(22) In the recognition scene Penelope has been criticised for her stubbornness, scepticism and caution, and Odysseus for his coldness and hard-heartedness. Is the scene psychologically convincing?

(23) Homer's Byzantine commentator Eustathius preserves the verdict of Aristarchus that the Homeric *Odyssey* ended at XXIII, 296 when Odysseus and Penelope retire to bed. Analysts have regarded the present ending as a late addition pointing to the following anomalies. Hermes is nowhere else in Homer seen in the role of 'psychopompos' (XXIV, 1–10). The White Rock is a puzzle (XXIV, 11). The unburied suitors enter Hades (the usual belief is that due burial rites are required before the spirit can pass to the underworld). Agamemnon and Achilles appear to meet for the first time (XXIV, 24). Amphimedon thinks that Odysseus prevailed upon Penelope to arrange the contest with the bow (XXIV, 167). This has been thought to be inconsistent with the actual narrative. No good reason can be found for the lies that Odysseus tells his father, or even for their meeting at all.

The allegorical tradition

When, early in the intellectual development of Greece, the first philosophers challenged the view of the world represented in the Homeric poems attacking the theology and sometimes the morality of Homer, his defenders resorted to allegorical interpretation, identifying beneath the literal surface meaning of Homer's words and fictions undermeanings (*hyponoiai*) which conformed to later notions about the nature of things. The story of Ares and Aphrodite told by Demodocus can be allegorised (somewhat fancifully) as follows. Hephaestus represents pure thought which is static so that he is lame. Ares and Aphrodite, representing strife and love, are caught and disciplined by the divine artificer. The gods laugh because they are really assisting Hephaestus in the creation of the universe. Many of the earliest allegories were physical. Allegorical interpretation was well established by the time of the philosopher Plato (*c.* 427–348 BC) who mistrusted it on the grounds that it is the literal meaning that makes the impression, and he believed that in their obvious meaning the Homeric poems misrepresented the nature of the divine and encouraged wrong attitudes and opinions about life. He therefore banished Homer from his ideal Republic believing the poems to be a bad influence upon the young. After Plato there were countless defenders of Homer who sought to prove in their commentaries that under the veil of fiction Homer was really a good philosopher.

The *Odyssey* more than the *Iliad* lends itself to this kind of interpretation. Here is the strongly moralised reading of the Roman poet Horace (65–8 BC):

Again, what virtue and wisdom can do, he has proposed Ulysses as an example for our instruction, he who tamed Troy and looked with discerning eyes upon the cities and manners of many men as he was planning a return for himself and his comrades; many difficulties he endured but could never be overborne by the waves of adversity. You know the Sirens' songs and the potions of Circe – if he had stupidly and greedily drunk these along with his companions he would have become the base and senseless slave of a harlot, he would have lived the life of a filthy dog or a sow that wallows in the mire. We are but ciphers, born merely to feed on the fruits of the earth, like the feckless suitors of Penelope...

(Epistles, I, 2, 17–28)

According to the traditional interpretation of the allegorisers, Odysseus, because of his wisdom, is able to enjoy pleasure but does not become a slave to it; he masters Circe, makes her his friend and sleeps with her without danger to himself. The episode becomes a lesson in temperance rather than abstinence. The Lotus-eaters and the Sirens represent different forms of the seductive temptation to hedonism and irresponsibility. In the Cyclops we see basic human savagery, the state of nature in which the individual will is not controlled and civilised by the social bond. In the main action the defeat of the greedy suitors, who are all excess and appetite, is accomplished by the man of control who uses his intelligence. This kind of interpretation can be reductive, of course; even the figures in the fabulous wanderings are presented in a more human way than this flat account of them suggests. Polyphemus for all his cruelty is nevertheless very fond of his favourite ram. But these undermeanings sometimes suggest underlying themes, implied meanings or archetypal patterns and help to explain the perennial appeal of the poem.

In a study of the famous translation of the *Odyssey* completed by George Chapman (*c*. 1559–*c*. 1634) in 1616, George de F. Lord* has convincingly argued that Chapman developed an individual version of the allegorical tradition whereby Odysseus triumphed over his external foes not merely through his superior wisdom but also by virtue of his own conquest of his self. According to this view Odysseus's decision to leave Calypso marks the beginning of the regeneration of the hero which is completed among the Phaeacians where he confesses past weaknesses in the course of his after-dinner narrative and rededicates himself to the domestic virtues represented by Arete. Having left Circe and Calypso, the obeisance before Arete marks Odysseus's return to the moral life so that he is now made worthy of Penelope. In some

---

* George de F. Lord, *Homeric Renaissance: The Odyssey of George Chapman*, Chatto & Windus, London, 1956.

allegorical accounts Scherie represents a life of pleasure itself to be renounced for rugged Ithaca; in this account it is something of an idealised version of the order that Odysseus must restore to Ithaca. Lord has argued that in this interpretation Chapman has brought out meanings that are present in the original. This is a bold claim and one that merits investigation and debate.

The allegorical tradition prompts the following questions: is Odysseus a virtuous man, and if so how is that virtue to be defined and in what does it chiefly consist? Is his wisdom worldly-wise and prudential or something more?

The *Odyssey* is not an allegorical epic like the *Faerie Queene* by Edmund Spenser (*c*. 1552−99) in which everyday realism and detail in the representation of persons and events are sacrificed in the interests of a clear moral and spiritual design. It is very difficult to read Spenser's poem without being conscious of such a design, which is deliberately transparent. But it is quite possible to read and enjoy the *Odyssey* at its narrative level without being directed from the realistic representation of life in some of its complexity, contradictoriness and variety to some definite interpretation of life embodied in that representation. Nevertheless the allegorical tradition is of interest to the modern student because it raises questions about the underlying meaning of the poem as a whole and the implied meaning or the thematic significance of particular episodes.

'Allegoria' in Greek simply means saying one thing in terms of another, and the sense in which it was used by the Greeks was not altogether precise. Homer tells us at the beginning of the *Odyssey* that the hero has incurred the wrath of Poseidon, that he is in the power of Calypso, a nymph who lives in a cave in a desert island. In Book V Zeus sends Hermes to free the hero from her clutches. In Book I Zeus tells us that he had sent Hermes to Aegisthus to warn him that Orestes would come and take vengeance if he attempted to usurp Agamemnon's throne. Later allegorists explain that Homer means that most of Odysseus's troubles come from the sea, that he has been living for seven years on a paradise island in hidden pleasure (Calypso in Greek means the Concealer) until reason asserts itself through the prompting of the mind. Similarly Aegisthus knew perfectly well, when he thought about it, what the consequences of his action would be. Not all the allegories are therefore absurd. When a modern cultural historian tells us that in archaic Greece Homer did not know how to represent psychological change without the use of the supernatural – that when, for example, Athene puts *menos* (strength) into Telemachus we are to interpret this as his way of showing that the youth summoned up the necessary inner resolution to face the suitors – he is a descendant of these early allegorists.

Comparison with the *Iliad*

The student of the *Odyssey* will naturally move on to compare the poem with the *Iliad*. The famous comparison in the ancient treatise *On the Sublime* attributed to the rhetorician Longinus and thought to have been written in the first century AD is a useful starting point:

> The *Odyssey* is an instance, how natural it is to a great genius, when it begins to grow old and decline, to delight itself in narrations and fables. For, that Homer composed the *Odyssey* after the *Iliad*, many proofs may be given ... From hence in my judgement it proceeds, that as the *Iliad* was written while his spirit was in its greatest vigour, the whole structure of that work is dramatic and full of action; whereas the greater part of the *Odyssey* is employed in narration, which is the taste of old age; so that in this latter piece we may compare him to the setting sun, which has still the same greatness but not the same ardour or force. He speaks not in the same strain; we see no more that *sublime* of the *Iliad* which marches on with a constant pace, without ever being stopped or retarded: there appears no more that hurry and that strong tide of motions and passions, pouring one after another: there is no more the same fury, or the same volubility of diction, so suitable to action, and all along drawing in such innumerable images of nature. But Homer, like the ocean, is always great, even when he ebbs and retires; even when he is lowest and loses himself most in narrations and incredible fictions; as instances of this we cannot forget the descriptions of tempests, the adventures of Ulysses with the Cyclops, and many others. But though all this be age, it is the age of Homer – and it may be said for the credit of these fictions, that they are beautiful dreams, or if you will, the dreams of Jupiter himself. I spoke of the *Odyssey* only to show, that the greatest poets when their genius wants strength and warmth for the pathetic, for the most part employ themselves in painting the manners. This Homer has done, in characterising the suitors, and describing their way of life; which is properly a branch of comedy, whose peculiar business it is to represent the manners of men.
>
> (IX, 11–15)

This translation of Longinus is taken from the postscript appended by the English neoclassicist Alexander Pope (1688–1744) to his own translation of the *Odyssey* published in 1724. Pope's rejoinder is worth reading in full; an extract is given here:

> Upon the whole, he affirms the *Odyssey* to have less sublimity and fire than the *Iliad*, but he does not say it wants the sublime or wants fire. He affirms it to be narrative, but not that the narration is defective. He affirms it to abound in fictions, not that those fictions are ill

invented, or ill executed. He affirms it to be nice and particular in painting the manners, but not that those manners are ill painted. If Homer has fully in these points accomplished his own design, and done all that the nature of his poem demanded or allowed, it still remains perfect in its kind, and as much a masterpiece as the *Iliad*.

The *Odyssey* ... ought to be considered according to its own nature and design, not with an eye to the *Iliad*.

The poems are markedly different in design. Both are epics but in the *Iliad* the Greeks regarded Homer as the father of tragedy, whereas in the *Odyssey* with its emphasis on character and its happy ending they regarded him as the father of comedy.

It has often been argued that the *Odyssey* represents a moral advance on the *Iliad* and that the Odyssean gods watch over the affairs of men with a more developed moral sense than their capricious Iliadic counterparts. In the opening of the poem Zeus gives the keynote speech which seems to put them on the side of justice. He rebukes men for blaming the gods for their misfortunes when it is only too apparent that they bring them upon themselves. Aegisthus is a case in point. The gods sent Hermes to warn that vengeance would come from Orestes if he usurped Agamemnon's throne. Later in the poem there is a divine presence of a kind not felt in the *Iliad*. When the companions of Odysseus have killed the cattle of the sun god, the forbidden flesh emits strange noises as it is being roasted. The mysterious light in the hall is attibuted to a divine presence. Athene constantly guards the protagonist and appears to him in person to assure him of continued protection. Yet Zeus does not say that all suffering comes to men through wrongdoing, nor does he say that when it is punished it is punished by the gods. The gods have foresight and warn Aegisthus, but they do not compel Orestes to do what he does. The point of the speech is to put the moral responsibility for action firmly upon men. The companions of Odysseus and the suitors die, like Aegisthus, through their own folly. In the *Iliad* the quarrel which leads to the catastrophe similarly results from the free action of Agamemnon and Achilles. The moments of supernatural mystery in the *Odyssey* are included primarily for poetic effect. The relationship between the goddess and the hero is based on the kind of personal affinity that underlies relations between men and gods in the *Iliad*. It could well be argued that the ingredients are basically the same in the poems but that they have been mixed differently to express a tragic vision in one, and to serve the interests of a poetic justice characteristic of comedy in the other.

Style and translation

In his lectures *On Translating Homer* (1861), the Victorian poet and critic Matthew Arnold (1822–88) offered his famous identification of four characteristic features of Homer's style and commented upon the difficulty which they presented to translators:

> the translator of Homer should above all be penetrated by a sense of four qualities of his author: – that he is eminently rapid; that he is eminently plain and direct, both in the evolution of his thought and the expression of it, that is, both in his syntax and in his words; that he is eminently plain and direct in the substance of this thought, that is, in his matter and ideas . . . And yet, in spite of this perfect plainness and directness of his ideas, he is eminently *noble*; . . . This is what makes his translators despair. 'To give relief' says Cowper [William Cowper (1731–1800) who translated Homer in the late eighteenth century] 'to prosaic subjects' (such as dressing, eating, drinking, harnessing, travelling, going to bed), that is to treat such subjects nobly, in the grand style, 'without seeming unseasonably tumid, is extremely difficult'. It *is* difficult, but Homer has done it. Homer is precisely the incomparable poet he is, because he has done it. His translation must not be tumid, must not be artificial, must not be literary; true; but then also he must not be commonplace, must not be ignoble.

Cowper and Arnold are reiterating an old truth about Homer's style. One of his ancient admirers writing in the last decades of the first century BC, Dionysius of Halicarnassus, quotes the opening lines of Book XVI in the third chapter of his treatise *On Literary Composition*, describing the scene in Eumaeus's hut and the reaction of his dogs at the moment when Telemachus returns, as an instance which illustrates Homer's ability to make enchanting poetry out of the simplest and most commonplace incidents of everyday life. Dionysius points out that all the words Homer uses here are quite ordinary, such as might be used by a farmer, a sailor or anyone who is not concerned with elegant speech. Neither is the language in the least figurative. When the lines are broken up, the language is utterly undistinguished. The beauty of the words derives from the order in which they are composed. The translators of this passage can be roughly divided into two kinds. Those in prose and recent translations in verse render the sense straightforwardly but the passage is reduced to its prosaic commonplace with all the enchantment of Homer's poetry utterly forsaken. Older verse translations aim to raise Homer above the level of prose, but in so doing resort to figurative language, special diction with an archaic flavour, or an artificial word order with the result that the natural simplicity and ease of the original is quite lost. There is no English translation of this passage worthy of quotation here. If these lines in Homer are used as a touchstone for judging translations, then the failure of all of them, including the most famous, is only too obvious.

Because of narrative passages like this, it was the experience of Alexander Pope that the *Odyssey* presented the translator with more difficulties than the *Iliad*:

> Accordingly the *Odyssey* is not always clothed in the majesty of verse proper to tragedy, but sometimes descends to plainer narrative, and sometimes even to that familiar dialogue essential to comedy. However, where it cannot support a sublimity, it always preserves a dignity or at least a propriety . . . Homer in his lowest narrations or speeches is ever easy, flowing, copious, clear and harmonious. He shows not less invention, in assembling the humbler, than the greater, thoughts and images; nor less judgement, in proportioning the style and versification to these, than to the other. Let it be remembered, that the same genius that soared the highest, and from whom the greatest models of the sublime are derived, was also he who stooped the lowest, and gave to the simplest narrative its utmost perfection. Which of these was the harder task to Homer himself, I cannot pretend to determine; but to his translator I can affirm (however unequal all his imitations must be) that of the latter has been much the more difficult.
>
> (Postscript to the *Odyssey*)

But the *Odyssey* is more than merely a succession of scenes of ordinary and commonplace experience. It is a poem of rich and varied texture; besides commonplace realism there is romantic adventure, and throughout a strong moral concern with memorable human episodes like the recognition scene between husband and wife. It would be surprising if the great translators failed to represent some of the many strengths of the original in their English recreations.

Here is Chapman's translation of the interview between Eurycleia and Telemachus on the night before he sets sail for Pylos and Sparta:

> Her, the prince did call,
> And said, 'Nurse! draw me the most sweete of all
> The wine thou keepst, next that which for my sire
> Thy care reserves, in hope he shall retire.
> Twelve vessels fill me forth, and stop them well.
> Then into well-sewd sacks, of fine ground meale
> Powre twentie measures. Nor to any one
> But thou thy selfe let this designe be knowne.
> All this see got together; I it all
> In night will fetch off, when my mother shall

Ascend her high roome and for sleepe prepare.
Sparta and Pylos I must see, in care
To find my father.' Out Euryclea cried,
And askt with teares: 'Why is your mind applied,
Deare sonne, to this course? Whither will you go?
So farre off leave us, and beloved so,
So onely? And the sole hope of your race?
Royall Ulysses, farre from the embrace
Of his kind countrie, in a land unknowne
Is dead, and you from your loved countrie gone,
The wooers will with some deceit assay
To your destruction, making then their prey
Of all your goods. Where in your owne y'are strong,
Make sure abode. It fits not you, so yong,
To suffer so much by the aged seas
And erre in such a waylesse wildernesse.'
   'Be cheared, loved nurse,' said he, 'for not without
The will of God go my attempts about.
Sweare therefore not to wound my mother's eares
With word of this before from heaven appeares
Th'eleventh or twelfth light, or her selfe shall please
To aske of me, or heares me put to seas –
Lest her faire bodie with her woe be wore.'
   To this the great oath of the Gods she swore;
Which having sworne, and of it every due
Performed to full, to vessels wine she drew,
And into well-sewd sacks powred foodie meale.
In meane time he (with cunning to conceale
All thought of this from others) himself bore
In broade house, with the wooers, as before.
(II, 348–81; Chapman, lines 522–61)

This is Pope's version of part of the Circe episode:

The palace in a woody vale they found,
High raised of stone; a shaded space around:
Where mountain wolves and brindled lions roam,
(By magic tamed) familiar to the dome.
With gentle blandishment our men they meet,
And wag their tails, and fawning lick their feet.
As from some feast a man returning late
His faithful dogs all meet him at the gate,
Rejoicing round, some morsel to receive,
(Such as the good man ever used to give.)
Domestic thus the grisly beasts drew near;

They gaze with wonder, not unmixed with fear.
Now on the threshold of the dome they stood,
And heard a voice resounding through the wood:
Placed at her loom within, the Goddess sung;
The vaulted roofs and solid pavement rung.
O'er the fair web the rising figures shine,
Immortal labour! worthy hands divine.
Polites to the rest the question moved,
(A gallant leader, and a man I loved.)
'What voice celestial, chanting to the loom
(Or nymph or goddess) echoes from the room?
Say shall we seek access?' With that they call;
And wide unfold the portals of the hall.
  The Goddess rising, asks her guests to stay,
Who blindly follow where she leads the way.
Eurylochus alone of all the band,
Suspecting fraud, more prudently remained.
On thrones around, with downy coverings graced,
With semblance fair th'unhappy men she placed.
Milk newly pressed, the sacred flower of wheat,
And honey fresh, and Pramnian wines the treat:
But venomed was the bread, and mixed the bowl,
With drugs of force to darken all the soul:
Soon in the luscious feast themselves they lost,
And drank oblivion of their native coast.
Instant her circling wand the Goddess waves,
To hogs transforms 'em, and the sty receives.
No more was seen the human form divine,
Head, face and members bristle into swine:
Still cursed with sense, their mind remains alone,
And their own voice affrights them when they groan.
Meanwhile the Goddess in disdain bestows
The mast and acorn, brutal food! and strows
The fruits of cornel, as their feast, around;
Now prone, and grovelling on unsav'ry ground.
                              (X, 210–43; Pope, lines 240–85)

The last interview of Telemachus and Menelaus Pope rendered thus:

But when the dawn bestreaked the east,
The king from Helen rose, and sought his guest.
As soon as his approach the hero knew,
The splendid mantle round him first he threw,
Then o'er his ample shoulders whirled the cloak,
Respectful met the monarch, and bespoke.

'Hail, great Atrides, favoured of high Jove!
Let not thy friends in vain for licence move.
Swift let us measure back the watery way,
Nor check our speed, impatient of delay.'
'If with desire so strong thy bosom glows,
Ill', said the king, 'should I thy wish oppose;
For oft in others freely I reprove
The ill-timed efforts of officious love;
Who love too much, hate in the like extreme,
And both the golden mean alike condemn.
Alike he thwarts the hospitable end,
Who drives the free, or stays the hasty friend;
True friendship's laws are by this rule expressed,
Welcome the coming, speed the parting guest.
Yet stay, my friends, and in your chariot take
The noblest presents that our love can make:
Meantime commit we to our women's care
Some choice domestic viands to prepare;
The traveller rising from the banquet gay,
Eludes the labours of the tedious way.
Then if a wider course shall rather please
Through spacious Argos, and the realms of Greece,
Atrides in his chariot shall attend;
Himself thy convoy to each royal friend.
No prince will let Ulysses' heir remove
Without some pledge, some monument of love;
These will the cauldron, these the tripod give,
From those the well-paired mules we shall receive,
Or bowl embossed whose golden figures live.'
(XV, 56–85; Pope, lines 65–99)

Cowper translated the warning of the disguised Odysseus to the suitors as follows:

hear me, therefore, mark me well.
Earth nourishes, of all that breathe or creep
No creature weak as man; for while the Gods
Grant him prosperity and health, no fear
Hath he, or thought, that he shall ever mourn;
But when the Gods with evils unforeseen
Smite him, he bears them with a grudging mind;
For such as the complexion of his lot
By the appointment of the Sire of all,
Such is the colour of the mind of man.
I, too, have been familiar in my day

With wealth and ease, but I was then self-willed,
And many wronged, emboldened by the thought
Of my own father's and my brethren's power.
Let no man, therefore, be unjust, but each
Use modestly what gift soe'er of heaven.
So do not these. These ever bent I see
On deeds injurious, the possessions large
Consuming, and dishonouring the wife
Of one, who will not, as I judge, remain
Long absent from his home, but is, perchance,
Ev'n at the door. Thee, therefore, may the Gods
Steal hence in time! ah, meet not his return
To his own country! for they will not part,
(He and the suitors) without blood, I think,
If once he enter at these gates again!
(XVIII, 129–50; Cowper, lines 158–83)

Let the reader compare these passages from Chapman, Pope and Cowper with other versions to assess their quality.

Specimen essay

What part is played in the structure of the Ithacan narrative by the fictional tales told by Odysseus?

Odysseus tells his first Cretan tale to Athene disguised as a young shepherd just after he has landed in Ithaca not knowing his whereabouts. When the shepherd tells him where he is, he thinks better of revealing himself and invents a story to explain his presence on the shore in the early morning with a quantity of treasure in an unknown place. He says that he is on the run, having killed Orsilochus the son of Idomeneus in an ambush because Orsilochus had tried to rob him of all the spoils he had won at Troy. Phoenician sailors had helped him to escape for a price and had been blown off course while making for Pylos depositing him instead on Ithaca with his treasure (XIII, 256–86). Athene smiles at Odysseus's tale and caresses him with her hand.

By the stratagem of the tale, which is a practical illustration of Odysseus's habitual inventiveness, caution and craft, the hero shows himself worthy of the attentions of the goddess who initiates the larger plan of the disguise. The tale also has its place in the characterisation of Odysseus, and the reaction of the goddess to it serves to clarify their natural affinity.

When he has arrived at Eumaeus's hut Odysseus is obliged to spin his second Cretan tale to give an account of himself and his condition to his host. He says that he is the son of a nobleman by his concubine who, despite having been slighted by his legitimate brothers, made a good marriage by virtue of his own natural qualities, for he is neither a fool nor a coward. He was once capable of great things and led many an ambush against foreign peoples. Before the Trojan War he had led nine such expeditions acquiring great wealth thereby. After Troy he stayed at home for only a month before he had the urge to set out on another expedition, this time to Egypt, where, because of the rash behaviour of his men, he almost lost his life in a battle with the natives, but when he threw himself on the mercy of their king, the latter spared him in deference to Zeus who protects strangers. Homer here links the tale to one of the great themes of the *Odyssey*. Odysseus goes on to say that he stayed in Egypt for seven years acquiring great wealth until he was prevailed upon by a cunning Phoenician to return with him to Phoenicia where he lived for a year, until the merchant made him go on an expedition to Libya with the secret intention of selling him into slavery. They were shipwrecked not far from Crete and only Odysseus lives to tell the tale. He landed in Thesprotia. The king's son escorted him to the palace and gave him a cloak and a tunic. At Thesprotia he learnt of Odysseus and saw his lost treasure awaiting his return from Dodona where he had gone to consult the oracle to see whether he should return to Ithaca openly or in disguise. The king put him on a ship for Dulichium but the crew plotted to sell him into slavery. They stripped him of his clothes and tied him up. He escaped while they were ashore eating, swam away and hid in a thicket by the shore. He then made his way to Eumaeus's hut (XIV, 199–359).

With this story Homer advances his plot in a number of ways. Eumaeus believes the tale except for the part relating to Odysseus and tells of the Aetolian stranger who came with tales of Odysseus's imminent return. Odysseus and the audience therefore learn that the Ithacans have been regaled with tales of their master's return before, so that realistic grounds are laid for caution and disbelief not only in Eumaeus but in Telemachus and later in Penelope herself. Secondly, in rebuking the stranger for trying to tell him (as he believes) what he wants him to hear, Eumaeus reveals his absolute moral worth. He is treating the stranger well not for any ulterior reason but out of uncontaminated respect for the laws of hospitality. In itself the tale introduces for the first time in the poem a motif that is to be replayed and varied for dramatic effect in the second half of the poem. The stranger regards the Trojan War as little more than one of a number of raiding expeditions which might be a source of potential wealth and good fortune. The emphasis in the tale is on the shifts in the fortune of the protagonist (often in the material sense) that result in his present exigency. The stranger later retells this tale in a shortened form to Antinous when he is begging from him where it serves as an exemplary warning to the fortunate not to ignore the plight of those who have fallen into misfortune (XVII, 419– 44). The same tale is told in a more abbreviated form a third time to the maid Melantho where again it is used to make a moral point (XIX, 71–88).

There follows the comic tale for which Odysseus (and Homer) almost apologises by means of which the stranger elicits a cloak from Eumaeus. On a night raid the stranger finds himself without a cloak. Odysseus the man of wit wakes up his men to ask one of them to take a message back to Agamemnon at the ships. Up jumps a volunteer and runs off, leaving behind his cloak for the stranger (XIV, 462–506). This is a further test of Eumaeus which he again passes with distinction. There is cunning in the crafty way in which the stranger recounts the craft of Odysseus. Homer's Odyssean wit is here humorously revealed.

The third Cretan tale is told by the stranger to Penelope just before the climactic decision to arrange the contest with the bow. The stranger pretends to be the younger brother of Idomeneus who entertained Odysseus on his way to Troy. Having gained Penelope's confidence by describing accurately the clothing Odysseus was wearing, he then assures her of her husband's imminent return, repeating the tale told to Eumaeus with the addition of the story of the loss of his companions after Thrinacie. He would have returned from the Phaeacians long ago, the stranger claims, had he not wished to travel about in pursuit of wealth (XIX, 172–202).

In the Cretan tales Odysseus consistently represents himself not as a heroic figure but as one who is motivated primarily by material considerations. The tales are the means by which he sustains his disguise as a beggar driven by want, and so, while being different in kind from the romantic and heroic tales within the first half of the poem, they are in accord with the demands of the more realistic Ithacan plot. They reveal Odysseus's wit and inventiveness, and they help to define and test the characters of the protagonists. Homer uses the tales, by exploiting the disguise for ironic effect, to ensure maximum human interest and to clarify his moral theme. At the same time the tales, even though they are known to be false, subtly suggest a wider context for the main action. The invented tales are not wholly unlike what purport to be the real histories of Theoclymenus and Eumaeus himself. Theoclymenus, formerly a wealthy man, is on the run as a result of a homicide. His story is one of disruption, loss of fortune, and migration (XV, 223–56). Eumaeus is the victim of piracy, greed and various forms of skulduggery (XV, 381–484). Penelope reminds Antinous that Odysseus had saved his father from pirates (XVI, 424–30). These tales and histories suggest a world not of heroic values but one dominated by the vagaries of fortune and by human greed. This is the backdrop to the reestablishment of order in Ithaca.

Part 5

Suggestions for further reading

The text and translations

HOMER: *Odyssey*, edited by T.W. Allen, 2 vols., Oxford Classical Texts, Clarendon Press, Oxford, 1917.

HOMER: *The Odyssey of Homer*, edited by W.B. Stanford, 2 vols., Macmillan, London and New York, 1948–50.

HOMER: *The Odyssey with an English Translation* by A.T. Murray, Loeb Classical Library, 2 vols., Heinemann, London; Harvard University Press, Cambridge, Massachusetts, 1919.

HOMER: *Iliad*, edited by T.W. Allen, 3 vols., Oxford Classical Texts, Clarendon Press, Oxford, 1931.

HOMER: *The Iliad with an English Translation* by A.T. Murray, Loeb Classical Library, 2 vols., Heinemann, London; Harvard University Press, Cambridge, Massachusetts, 1924.

HOMER: *The Odyssey*, translated by E.V. Rieu, Penguin Books, Harmondsworth, 1946.

HOMER: *The Iliad*, translated by E.V. Rieu, Penguin Books, Harmondsworth, 1950.

CHAPMAN, GEORGE: *Chapman's Homer*, edited by Allardyce Nicoll, Volume Two, *The Odyssey*, Routledge & Kegan Paul, London, 1957.

COWPER, WILLIAM: *The Odyssey of Homer*, Everyman's Library, J.M. Dent, London, 1910.

POPE, ALEXANDER: *Translations of Homer: The Odyssey*, edited by Maynard Mack (Vols. IX and X of *The Twickenham Edition of the Poems of Alexander Pope*, general editor, John Butt), Methuen, London; Yale University Press, New Haven, 1967.

Works of general reference

Atlas of Ancient and Classical Geography, Everyman's Library, J.M. Dent, London, 1950.

A Companion to Homer, edited by A.J.B. Wace and F.H. Stubbings, Macmillan, London, 1962.

A Dictionary of Greek and Roman Biography and Mythology, edited by W. Smith, 3 vols., London, 1876.

FINLEY, M.I.: *The World of Odysseus*, Penguin Books, Harmondsworth, 1962.

The Oxford Classical Dictionary, edited by N.G.L. Hammond and H.H. Scullard, 2nd edition, Clarendon Press, Oxford, 1970.

SCHERER, M.R.: *The Legends of Troy in Art and Literature*, Phaidon Press, London and New York, 1963.

Criticism of Homer

ARISTOTLE: *Aristotle's Theory of Poetry and Fine Art*, translated with critical notes by S.H. Butcher, 3rd edition, Edinburgh, 1902.

ARNOLD, MATTHEW: *Matthew Arnold: On the Classical Tradition*, edited by R.H. Super, University of Michigan Press, Ann Arbor, 1960. Contains his lectures 'On Translating Homer'.

'LONGINUS': *Aristotle: The Poetics; 'Longinus': On the Sublime: Demetrius: On Style*, Loeb Classical Library, Heinemann, London; Harvard University Press, Cambridge, Massachusetts, 1932.

LORD, G. DE F.: *Homeric Renaissance: The Odyssey of George Chapman*, Chatto & Windus, London, 1956.

MASON, H.A.: *To Homer Through Pope: An Introduction to Homer's Iliad and Pope's Translation*, Chatto & Windus, London, 1972. Contains a chapter on modern translations of the *Odyssey*.

STANFORD, W.B.: *The Ulysses Theme: A Study in the Adaptability of a Traditional Hero*, 2nd edition, Basil Blackwell, Oxford, 1963.

The author of these notes

ROBIN SOWERBY was educated at St Catharine's College Cambridge, where he read Classics and English. Since 1972 he has been a lecturer in the Department of English Studies at Stirling University. He is also the author of York Notes on *The Iliad*, *The Aeneid* and *The Republic*.